EXPLORING
ASHDOWN FOREST

Eight Circular Walks and Two Motor Tours

David Harrison

S.B. Publications

By the same author:
Exploring Brighton and the South Downs
Exploring Eastbourne and the South Downs
The South Downs Way

To Mick Brownhill

First published in 1998 by S.B. Publications
c/o 19 Grove Road, Seaford, East Sussex BN25 1TP

ISBN 1 85770 162 3

Typeset, printed and bound by
MFP Design & Print
Longford Trading Estate,
Thomas Street,
Stretford,
Manchester.
M32 0JT

CONTENTS

	page
EXPLORING THE ASHDOWN FOREST	4
THE ASHDOWN FOREST — A SHORT HISTORY	5
— CROWBOROUGH	7
MOTOR TOUR — ONE (39.5mile/64.3km) Crowborough -Kings Standing - Gills Lap - Ashdown Forest Centre - Weir Wood Reservoir - Forest Row - Colemans Hatch - Hartfield - Withyham - Groombridge - High Rocks - Frant - Rotherfield - Crowborough	9
MOTOR TOUR - TWO (48mile/78.3km) Crowborough - Fairwarp - Maresfield - Barkham Manor Vineyards - Fletching - Newick - Wivelsfield - Chailey - Sheffield Park Station (Bluebell Railway) - Sheffield Park Gardens - Heaven Farm - Danehill - Horsted Keynes - Nutley (Windmill) - Crowborough	28
WALK 1 - Pooh Walk (8.5mls/14km) or (5mls/8km)	49
WALK 2 - The Priest House (6mls/10km)	53
WALK 3 - Roman Road (8mls/12.8km)	57
WALK 4 - Airman's Grave (6.5mls/10.7km)	62
WALK 5 - Piltdown (8.5mls/14km)	67
WALK 6 - Wivelsfield (4.25mls/7km) or (3mls/4.8km)	70
WALK 7 - The Chaileys (8mls/12.8km)	75
WALK 8 - Horsted Keynes (6mls/10km)	80

Front Cover: Looking north east towards Hartfield, one mile from the Ashdown Forest Centre

Back Cover: Nutley post-mill

Title Page: Pooh Bridge

Photographs by Tony Bannister

EXPLORING THE ASHDOWN FOREST

Most people have probably never even heard of the Ashdown Forest let alone know where it is. Pooh Bear addicts will know, of course, or at least will be aware of some of its locations, and Walk 1 on page 49 will certainly bring the Enchanted Place and Pooh Bridge to life, but what else has this fascinating part of East Sussex got to offer? Well at 6400 acres it isn't very big for one thing - although in ancient times it spread over twice its present area — and this accounts for why several of the villages on its present outer extremities were once part of the original forest and are included as such in this exploration. It doesn't have all that many trees as forests go, but what it does have is an outstanding beauty all of its own that entices the visitor to explore further into its hidden charm with surprising consequences. For within its confines are delightful villages simply oozing with history; gardens so picturesque and photogenic to be known all over the world; the oldest working windmill in the county and a railway that is legendary in the annuls of steam preservation.

Ashdown Forest attracts visitors for any number of reasons. Horseriders have countless bridleways throughout the forest from which they are able to enjoy their freedom within the intricate network of routes available to them. Walkers have virtual freedom of the entirety of the forest and there are countless number of car parks available from which to start exploring. The Forest Centre has leaflets available outlining short walks from several car parks dotted throughout the forest and details describing 8 walks of varying duration and differing locations appears at the end of this book.

So prepare to experience a part of Sussex completely different from the rest of the county; discover the location of one of the world's greatest hoaxes: wander through the regions best known vineyards: see the lakes and hammer ponds that once were part of a rich iron industry: witness the lonely and fitting memorial to the crew of a Wellington bomber that crashed in the forest during the Second World War.

Two drives take in the whole of the area of the forest. Not all of Ashdown Forest is accessible by public services so without transport a full exploration will be difficult. The area it covers is small enough to consider cycling to the remote areas or failing that everywhere is accessible on foot, but either of these methods of exploration will require detailed planning that is not included in this guide.

Whichever way an exploration is made it is guaranteed to leave a lasting impression. Ashdown Forest *is* different from anywhere else. From the moment you set foot in its confines you will begin to see why!

ASHDOWN FOREST - A SHORT HISTORY

Not so much a forest as a heath these days, for if it is trees standing in plantations you are expecting to see then venture forward with an open mind and accept the area for what it is and not what you would like it to be. For this last major untamed fragment of a vast expanse of woodland that was known to the Romans as *Anderida* is part of Andreadsweald or Andredesweald, the great Saxon Forest which stretched from Kent to Hampshire across most of Southern England, though it may well have been a comparatively bald patch in that mighty oakwood.

In fact there are several patches of birchwood, a few oaks and some splendid groups of pine, but in the main the Forest is to be enjoyed for its openness, its wide green droves, undulating sandy hills and total freedom to enjoy all its beauty and amenities. In short the Forest is a walkers' paradise, with several route-marked walks and leaflets available from a well designed Forest Centre explaining all about the flora and fauna en route (see page 15).

The walks referred to today are totally different to the *walks* of several centuries ago however. In medieval England when the Forest was known as Lancaster Great Park, Edward III granted it to his third son John of Gaunt, Duke of Lancaster, who owned it between 1372-1399. Then its prime purpose was for hunting, not only for food but for sport as well. Red and fallow deer thrived on the habitat and the Forest was enclosed by a *pale*, a bank surmounted by a wooden fence with a parallel internal ditch. This made it easy for the deer to jump into the Forest but virtually impossible for them to jump out. They were managed by keepers and foresters in each of the six *walks* of the Forest - for a *walk* in those days was an administrative division of the Forest, so the forester was rather like a policeman covering a beat (or *walk*) today.

As the forester was also responsible for other duties within the county and at court, he had a deputy to oversee the activities of the commoners who had legal rights to the Forest, to graze their animals and collect wood for their fires. This deputy would be responsible to oversee large stretches of the Forest which he would *range* on horseback, thus the Ranger became evident in our vocabulary in much the same way as we know him today. Anyone found breaking the Forest's laws would be called before the *Woodmote* or Wood Court and would most probably be fined.

IRON INDUSTRY

The Forest has been associated with the iron industry since man began to hack clearings in the Iron Age (600BC-AD43) and the Romans helped accelerate the process. They drove their road from London to Lewes through the heart of the Weald and visual evidence can still be seen of this (see page 60).

The Romans then the Saxons and medieval man dug ironstone from the clay of the lower-lying land then felled trees to provide charcoal for their smelting furnaces. The water power needed came from ponds formed by damming streams and most of the streams in the Forest today are still discoloured with the reddiness of iron.

By the sixteenth century this part of Sussex was providing most of Britain's iron, which was proving to be of vital importance because the Nation's cannon were cast from it. Come the early nineteenth century and the Wealden iron industry was in rapid decline. With most of the timber of the Forest gone there was little wonder the industry disappeared, but even though this has been considered the main reason for deforestisation it is unlikely to have been the only cause. Records show that the sixteenth century was the zenith of operations in the Ashdown Forest with no fewer than 32 furnaces in operation in this part of Sussex alone. If this were the case then all the trees cut down would have been regenerated, leaving an even thicker forest than before. It is much more likely that all the grazing animals belonging to the commomers polished off the trees, with nobody replanting in their wake.

SMUGGLERS

Iron workers and charcoal burners were not the only industrious occupations of the Forest inhabitants. Its bleak and often isolated depths gave shelter to poachers, horse thieves and smugglers, whose trains of pack-horses would come up in the darkness of night along devious routes from the coast, unknown to the otherwise diligent excisemen. The scattered hamlet of Duddleswell was always a notorious haunt of poachers and smugglers and one of their trails led over Camp Hill to Nutley.

HUNTING

The ancient boundaries of the Forest embraced an area of 14000 acres though this has been drastically reduced since half of it was enclosed in the early eighteenth century. It took several Acts of Parliament to retain the remaining 6400 acres as common land which is now governed by a Board of Conservators and designated an area of Special Scientific interest.

It was visited regularly by keen royal huntsmen such as Henry VIII and James I, although the lack of interest in the area was evident in the reign of Charles I, resulting in the loss of deer stocks during the Intervegnum. The Forest's final collapse as a hunting park came with the Civil War, when the Master Forester and his Rangers supported the lost Cavalier cause and the area along with four other former Royal forests was handed to the parliamentary army in part settlement of their arrears in pay. It has taken almost 300 years for deer to return to the Forest in significant numbers and almost as long for the legal rights of commoners to retain access to land which had been theirs by right since Saxon times.

In 1974 a new Act of Parliament gave the public the right of access to wander on foot over the whole of the Forest which is now owned by the Ashdown Forest Trust.

Today fire is the Forest's major concern. One careless human act and much of what remains of the Forest could be wiped out overnight. The Ashdown Forest is now there for everyone to enjoy. Use it but do not abuse it. Take great care not to start a fire - it could kill far more than just trees and heathland!

CROWBOROUGH

Once, because it was well wooded and not over populated, and because it was geographically situated on the main smuggler's route from the coast to East Grinstead, Crowborough was deemed the ideal place for hiding contraband goods until it was considered necessary to move them on. Mead House, with its numerous outbuildings, was considered to be one of the most popular places for storing illicit goods.

The Crowborough Cross Hotel's present premises date from the seventeenth century when it was called the Red Cross Inn, but records show that there was an earlier wooden building on the same site which was an alehouse in the sixteenth century. Its name the Red Cross Inn was due to the four coaches a week that past it doors in the eighteenth and nineteenth centuries. There were no road maps in those days and the coachmen had to find their way with the aid of a three inch wide drawing of the road which they rotated on rollers as they passed each landmark as they went along. Each stage of the route would have a symbol which the coachmen would follow and the crossroads in Crowborough would have been marked on their drawing with a red cross.

Although the interior of the inn has been altered considerably since its coaching days there is still evidence of its historic past.

Today Crowborough is mainly commuter belt country with nothing else of any great age — even the church is eighteenth century, though it does have a rare reredos, a tribute to the taste and skill of the ladies of this place for they carved it themselves through three years of loving labour.

It is from Crowborough we begin two motor tours of the Ashdown Forest, starting and finishing at the crossroads.

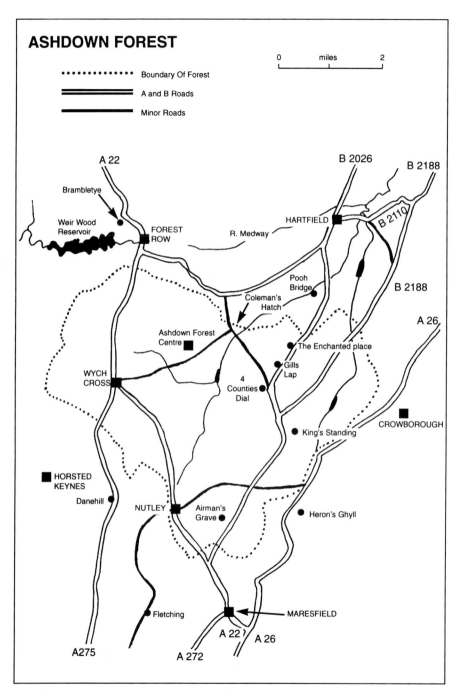

MOTOR TOUR — ONE
(39.5MILE/64.3KM)

CROWBOROUGH — KING'S STANDING — GILLS LAP — ASHDOWN FOREST CENTRE — WEIR WOOD RESERVOIR — FOREST ROW — COLEMANS HATCH — HARTFIELD — WITHYHAM — GROOMBRIDGE — HIGH ROCKS — FRANT — ROTHERFIELD — CROWBOROUGH

1. Crowborough to King's Standing (4.5mile/7.6km)

Leave the crossroads westward taking the first left signposted Horder Centre for Arthiritis and in 2 mile (3.3km) turn left onto the B2188 signposted Maresfield. In a further 2.5 mile (4.3km) reach Kings Standing car park on the left.

No toilets or refreshment facilities available here.

2. King's Standing to Gills Lap (1mile/1.6km)

Turn right out of car park taking left fork signposted Hartfield to Gills Lap car park on the left.

No toilets or refreshment facilities available here.

3. Gills Lap to Ashdown Forest Centre (3.25mile/5.4km)

Leave Gills Lap on the minor road to Coleman's Hatch, turning left by the Hatch Inn signposted Wych Cross. The Ashdown Forest Centre car park is off to the right 1.25mile (2km) along this road.

Toilets (including disabled facilities) available. Refreshments at Wych Cross Nurseries, Garden Centre Tea Rooms 1mile (1.6km) on towards Wych Cross.

4. Ashdown Forest Centre to Weir Wood Reservoir (4mile/6.6km)

Turn right out of Forest Centre to the crossroads at Wych Cross. Cross straight over signposted Sharpthorne to second crossroads in 1.25mile (2km). Keep straight ahead again for a further 1.75mile (2.8km) and the Reservoir car park is on the right.

No toilets or refreshment facilities available here.

5. Weir Wood Reservoir to Forest Row (4.25mile/7km)

Turn left out of car park and return the 1.75mile (2.8km) to crossroads, where turn left signposted Forest Row. Turn right in Forest Row onto A22

MOTOR TOUR - ONE

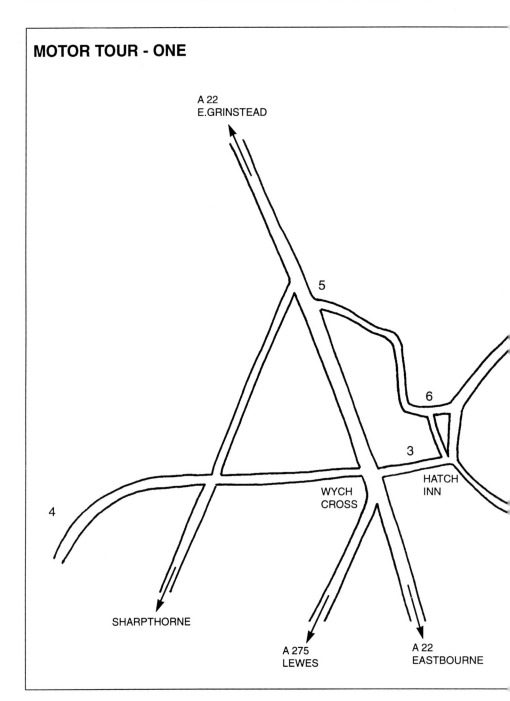

A 22
E.GRINSTEAD

5

6

3

HATCH
INN

WYCH
CROSS

4

SHARPTHORNE

A 275
LEWES

A 22
EASTBOURNE

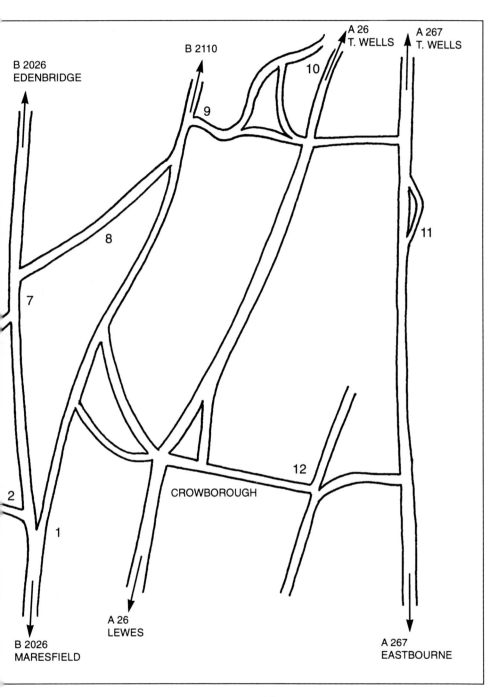

then left at mini roundabout onto B2110 signposted Hartfield. Car park behind Foresters Arms on left or a little further along on the right.
   Toilets and refreshment facilities available here.

6. Forest Row to Coleman's Hatch (2mile/3.3km)

Keep ahead along the B2110 where there is adequate parking in a layby immediately beyond Coleman's Hatch church.
   Toilets and refreshment facilities available at the Hatch Inn 0.5mile (0.8km) down the road opposite the church.

7. Coleman's Hatch to Hartfield (2mile/3.3km)

Continue along the B2110 into Hartfield where there is plenty of parking alongside the road through the village.
   Toilets and refreshment facilities available here.

8. Hartfield to Withyham (1.5mile/2.3km)

Follow the B2110 to the right as it leaves the village for Withyham where there is parking behind the church.
   Toilets and refreshment facilities at the Dorset Arms at the entrance to Buckhurst Park

9. Withyham to Groombridge (3mile/4.8km)

Turn right back onto the B2110 into Groombridge. Turn sharp right at the Victoria public house then left into the car park.
   Toilets and refreshments available here.

10. Groombridge to High Rocks (2.5mile/4km)

Turn left out of car park and left again at sign to Tunbridge Wells/Frant. Left again in 1 mile (1.6km) at sign for High Rocks. Large car park on right immediately before High Rocks Inn.
   Toilets and refreshments available here.

11. High Rocks to Frant (3.5mile/5.6km)

Left out of car park and left again at Fairview Lane. Turn left at T-junction signposted Frant to A26 where turn right then left at staggered crossroads signposted Frant. Turn right onto A267 into Frant and in little over half a mile (1km) turn off left signposted Frant church where there is limited parking available.
   Toilets and refreshments available here.

12. Frant to Rotherfield (5mile/8km)

Return to A267 signposted Heathfield and in 3mile (4.8km) turn right onto B2100 signposted Crowborough. In 2mile (3.2km) turn right at the T-

junction in Rotherfield where parking is available by the church.
   Toilets and refreshments available here.

13. Rotherfield to Crowborough (3mile/4.8km)

Follow the B2100 back into Crowborough to conclude the tour..

Old Town Hall, Forest Row

POINTS OF INTEREST DURING THE TOUR

1. King's Standing

It was here that a raised hide was situated, presumably in the clump still visible, which became a feature of the type of hunting that became popular in late Tudor times. The *Standing,* or raised shooting box, was a tall open-sided structure from which the royal and noble huntsmen would be esconced. For instead of the old familiar method of chasing deer on horseback the hunters would shoot with bow and arrow or gun at the deer as they were driven past the *Standing* by keepers.

A similar *Standing* survives to this day at Chingford in Epping Forest. There are no toilets or refreshment facilities here.

Public Transport: No public transport passes Kings Standing.

2. Gills Lap

This is Pooh Bear country. Winnie the Pooh, immortalised by A.A. Milne, was inspired by the author's perambulations in the Forest and many of the locations referred to in his books were based on actual places hereabouts, particularly Lone Pine and the Enchanted Place.

There are no toilets or refreshment facilities here.

King's Standing

Public Transport: *No public transport passes Gills Lap.*

Walk: *A walk of 8.5mile (14km) which can be shortened to 5mile (8km) quite easily without missing any of the salient points begins from the car park, visiting Pooh Bridge and other Pooh locations. The longer version also includes Pooh Corner and Hartfield although these are visited in the Motor Tour (see page 20).*

3. Ashdown Forest Centre

An information centre housed within three reconstructed thatched medieval barns. Inside is a small exhibition relating to the forest, telling of some of the work being carried out to help preserve and protect the animals, birds, insects and fauna that live in the forest.

Also available are leaflets describing short walks from several of the Forest car parks and a detailed map of the area is also a useful asset.

Toilets (including disabled facilities) available at the Forest Centre. Refreshments available at Wych Cross Nurseries, Garden Centre Tea Rooms 1mile (1.6km) on towards Wych Cross.

Hours of Opening: *Open all year weekends and public holidays 11-5 and weekdays in the summer 2-5 Tel: 01342 823583*

Weir Wood Reservoir

Information Board, Weir Wood Reservoir

Public Transport: There is no direct public transport from Crowborough. Route 729 operates an hourly service to Uckfield where Route 261 connects with 3 buses (Monday to Saturdays only) direct to the Forest Centre with return via the same route. Check bus times before travelling.

4. Weir Wood Reservoir

Built in 1954 and owned by Southern Water, the Reservoir is home to mallard, coot and moorhen while the cormorant is a regular visitor from the nearby coast. In springtime the great crested grebe is a popular visitor while in the autumn osprey from Scotland stop off here to feed and rest before their long migratory haul to Africa.

No toilet or refreshment facilites available here.

Public Transport: No public transport passes Weir Wood Reservoir.

Walk: A splendid 6mile (10km) circuit criss-crossing the Bluebell Line, passing within sight of the majestic Gravetye Manor and visiting the charming village of West Hoathly with its Priest House Museum. (See page 53).

5. Forest Row

The gateway to Ashdown Forest; for it was here the hunting lodges were

Old Town Hall, Forest Row

Brambletye Manor

Brambletye Hotel, Forest Row

built to house the royal hunting parties after a hard day in the saddle and it was not until the railway was opened in 1866 that there was any substantial development in the area, achieving full parish status in 1894. The railway is no more and the track has been turned into a country trail. On its eastward section towards East Grinstead it passes the ruins of Brambletye House, built in 1631 for Sir Henry Compton. Half a century later it was owned by Sir James Richards who, while out hunting one day in the Forest, was warned that he was suspected of treason and that his house was to be searched. He took immediate flight to the coast, taking a boat to Spain and returning to Brambletye no more. It is said that since that day when Sir James passed through the gatehouse the house has never been tenanted since. Horace Smith renewed interest in the place with his famous historical romance in 1826, a book much admired by Sir Walter Scott, and the name lives on in the Brambletye Hotel which was featured in Sir Arthur Conan Doyle's *Black Peter* when Sherlock Holmes spent some time here. The hotel has a 'Black Peter's Bar' to this day.

Another interesting building is Kidbrooke Park, built in 1724 for Lord Abergavenny after his Eridge Park estate was destroyed by fire. It has seen many owners, including Charles Abbot, Speaker of the House of Commons at the beginning of the nineteenth century and Olaf Hambro, chairman of Hambros Bank who bought the house in 1921. He helped finance an expedition to the Himalayas by Kingdon-Ward who brought back a blue poppy which the late Queen Mary, wife of GeorgeV, came to Forest Row to see. Hambro sold the house in 1938 after the death of his wife and it became a school. It is not open to public view.

Another educational establishment given the royal seal of approval was Ashdown House preparatory school, when it was chosen by Princess Margaret and Lord Snowdon for their son Viscount Linley, and the couple were regular visitors to the village while he was a pupil there.

Toilets and refreshment facilities available at several venues in the village.

Public Transport: No direct service from Crowborough. Route 729 to Tunbridge Wells operates hourly (Monday to Saturday) and 2 hourly on Sundays with connecting service Route 291 to Forest Row every 2 hours (except Sunday). Check times of buses before travelling.

6. Colemans Hatch

The name goes back to 1279 after Edmund and Richard Coleman when *'hatch'* signified a gate. The hamlet is on the edge of Ashdown Forest and here would have been one of seven original gates or *'hatches'* to the forest.

The splendid church dates from 1913, built by John McAndrew of Holly Hill, the principal property in the area, who until then had been Churchwarden at nearby Hartfield. Opposed to the introduction of high-church practices by the Rev W Beckles, incumbent at Hartfield (1905-20), Mc Andrew sought permission from the Bishop to build the new church and thus endow a new parish. It has a dozen attractive stained glass windows depicting over a hundred different figures in them, but its finest possession is a magnificent copy of a famous Italian Pieta, the one by Francesco Francia in the National Gallery, which probably explains why it is kept locked.

Toilets and refreshments

Colemans Hatch Church

available from the Hatch Inn half a mile (0.8km) down the road opposite the church.

Public Transport: No direct service from Crowborough. Route 729 to Tunbridge Wells operates hourly (Monday to Saturday) and 2 hourly on Sundays with connecting service Route 291 to Colemans Hatch every 2 hours (except Sunday). Check times of buses before travelling.

7. Hartfield

Mentioned in the Domesday Book, there was almost certainly a church here before the present church of St Mary was built around the middle of the thirteenth century, with added constructions, rebuilding and alterations of a material nature almost every century since.

This would have been hunting country, although it was a centre of the important iron industry prevelent in the area, with the river Medway the main route in and out of the village for heavy wares. The Romans were no stranger to the village, for they built a road nearby with visual evidence still visible (see page 60). But it was the writer A.A. Milne who immortalised the place, with his tales of *"Winnie the Pooh"* and there is a shop dedicated to his characters in the high street.

The lychgate leading to the church is interesting and much photographed for it is formed by an old yew tree and an ancient timbered cottage. In the graveyard, near to the porch, is the tomb of Nicholas

Lychgate, Hartfield

"Beggarman" Smith who died 300 years ago leaving a small fortune. During his life he resolved to find out the nature of Sussex folk by disguising himself as a tramp. Wandering from village to village as a beggar he came across little kindness until he came to Hartfield and he remembered the village in his will. On each Good Friday since his death the poor of the village congregate around his grave to receive his bounty from the rector and churchwardens, and still the practice continues to this day.

There are three inns in the village each with a fascinating tale to tell. The **Anchor Inn**, before it became an inn a century ago, was originally the workhouse for women under the control of the Hartfield Board of Guardians. Their control must have been pretty strict, for in a recent renovation at the inn ankle chains were discovered, presumably to restrict the movements of more wayward inmates.

In 1781 the **Haywaggon Inn** was called the Dorset Arms and it did not change to its present name until the 1960's when it was sold by Earl de la Warr's estate. Lodging there in 1820 a Mr Artherford lost six pounds and a notice was erected in the village advertising a reward for its return. The penalty for stealing by finding in those days was death! Records show that nobody was convicted for the crime so presumably Mr Artherford got his money back.

A little way out of the village on the road to Colemans Hatch is the **Gallipot Inn**. Consisting of three almshouses built by the parish for its

Gallipot Inn, Hartfield

poor in the sixteenth century they were later occupied by three brothers. In one lived Jack who made shoes for the gentry and clogs for the workers. In the second lived William who brewed beer and cider and in the third lived Albert who made small glazed jars used for medicines called gallipots. When his brothers died William converted all three cottages into an inn and it has been a free house ever since.

Toilets and refreshments available at the three aforementioned inns.

Public Transport: No direct service from Crowborough. Route 729 to Tunbridge Wells operates hourly (Monday to Saturday) and 2 hourly on Sundays with connecting service Route 291 to Hartfield every 2 hours (except Sunday). Check times of buses before travelling.

Walk: A delightful 8mile (12.8km) walk visiting a stretch of Roman road at Holtye before returning through woodland to Bolebroke Castle and back along the old railway. (See page 57.)

8. Withyham

Although not mentioned in Domesday Book the name implies a Saxon settlement and records show that it was in existence around the time of the Norman Conquest. Certainly the estate of Buckhurst was in the hands of the Sackville family from 1200 and has remained so to present day, a

Church porch, Withyham

span of 800 years, a record few other families could ever hope to equal. By 1291 there was mention of a church here, which during the fourteenth century was almost completely rebuilt only to be destroyed by fire on 16th June 1663 having been struck by lightning. Within ten years it had been rebuilt again with the Sackville Chapel completed by 1680. It was to this place the Sackvilles were brought, wherever they died, to be buried in vaults beneath the chapel while monuments to their memory remain for all to see, none more noble than Caius Gabriel Cibber's masterpiece to young Thomas Sackville, who was only thirteen when he died in 1675 at Samur on the river Loire in France. The life size marble figures of his parents kneeling on cushions and gazing sadly at the reclining boy holding a skull, symbolising death in infancy, are frozen in everlasting grief, for in less than two years the boy's father had also died, leaving his mother to commission the monument commemorating her husband and all her children.

The great Park of Buckhurst was the original home of the Sackvilles before Sir Thomas Sackville, Lord Buckhurst, was created 1st Earl of Dorset in 1567, a year after he had been granted the Manor of Knole in Kent, a house famous even then in its own right, and still in the Sackville family today. His descendant the 5th Duke had no heir, so his estate passed to his sister, Lady Elizabeth Sackville, who married the 5th Earl de la Warr, and it is this branch of the family who still owns Buckhurst today.

The private drive to the right of the Dorset Arms is a public right of way and it is well worth strolling through the Park with its beautiful beeches, lakes and vistas until the chimneys of Buckhurst Place become visible when the footpath turns off sharp left as the way ahead becomes private property. This is the cue to retrace steps back to the Dorest Arms for a spot of lunch or light refreshment.

Little remains of the original Buckhurst Place which was largely destroyed in 1690. A new house built on the same site as the old in Tudor style in 1738 was Victorianized in 1884 and given a new Lutyens wing in 1900. It has a sunken garden with a lake fed by two streams of the nearby Medway and fascinating glens among its ancient beeches.

Toilets and refreshments available at the Dorset Arms.

Public Transport: No direct service from Crowborough. Route 729 to Tunbridge Wells operates hourly (Monday to Saturday) and 2 hourly on Sunday with connecting service Route 291 to Withyham every 2 hours (except Sunday). Check times of buses before travelling.

9. Groombridge

The old village dates back to Saxon times when *Gromenbregge*, the fortification by the Grom, defended this outpost of the kingdom of Kent

Groombridge Place

— for indeed the village is split by the River Medway, the northern bank being in Kent and the southern bank in Sussex. A picturesque group of sixteenth to eighteenth century cottages surround the green and its beautiful church houses the remains of one of our greatest heroes, William Cotton Oswell, to whom there is a marble tablet over the door. He accompanied Livingstone in some of his most stirring adventures and had more hair raising escapes than any man alive. He would hunt elephant on foot and was twice tossed by a rhinoceros but Livingstone considered him to be one of his most trusted and courageous friends.

Groombridge Place was built in 1662 on earlier foundations and its beautiful gardens owe much to the interest of John Evelyn who often used to visit here. It was from here the renowned soldier Sir Richard Waller set off with Henry V to Agincourt where he captured Charles of Orleans, a brother of the King of France. He was brought back to Groombridge Place and kept captive for 25 years, not here as is widely believed, but in many places, including the Tower of London. It was John, Charles' younger son, who was a prisoner at Groombridge, held as hostage which proved so profitable that Sir Richard was able to rebuild Groombridge Place.

The house is not open to the public but the gardens are.

Toilets and refreshments available in the village.

Hours of Opening: April-October 9am-6pm (or dusk if earlier)

Public Transport: No direct service from Crowborough. Route 729 to Tunbridge Wells operates hourly (Monday to Saturday) and 2 hourly on Sundays with connecting service Route 291 to Groombridge every 2 hours (except Sunday).   Route 290 operates a Limited Stop service between Tunbridge Wells and Groombridge (except Sundays) on a more regular basis.   Check times of both services before travelling.

10. High Rocks

Perhaps the biggest formation of sandstone rocks in the area it is easy to see why they are so popular as a training ground for mountaineers and used as the headquarters of the Sandstone Climbing Club of Great Britain.

An admission charge may be made for entry.

Toilets and refreshments available.

Public Transport: No public transport passes High Rocks

11. Frant

The name originates from the Anglo-Saxon *Fern-ethe* meaning ferny heath, for it is situated on a high ridge with splendid views over the surrounding countryside. By the middle of the sixteenth century the area became increasingly prosperous thanks to profits from iron smelting and gun founding and an improved stone church was built in the village. Following the demise of the iron industry, Frant became heavily involved in smuggling until well into the eighteenth century, when very few families in the area escaped the stigma of poverty. The Napoleonic Wars intensified the situation with the majority of the population unemployed and poorly housed, and it was inevitable riots developed with condemned offenders imprisoned or transported to Australia.

The church was rebuilt in 1821 and extended in 1867 and most of its possessions are memorials to a variety of residents. Hans Busk lies under a tall monument; he was the originator of the Territorial Army after impressing on Lord Melbourne the importance of rifle clubs and a volunteer army. A memorial tablet to Colonel John By of the Royal Engineers tells of the Peninsular War veteran who went out to Canada to supervise the construction of canals. In 1826 he founded Bytown, later to become Ottawa, and was much criticised for overspending his canal budget that he retired to Frant seeking sanctuary at Shernford Park, a house once bought by Richard Budgen, who by 1724 had made a large scale survey of the whole of Sussex, for he was a surveyor and mapmaker.

A large obelisk in the churchyard is in the memory of Stratford Canning, Lord Stratford de Redcliffe, one of the greatest diplomats of the nineteenth century. Serving four sovereigns he was an experienced diplomat well before Waterloo and while ambassador in Turkey negotiated single-handed the treaty of Bukarest in 1812 between Russia and Turkey. He exercised his influence to effect internal reforms in Turkey, safeguarding the rights of Christians and became so closely connected with Turkish policy that when nominated ambassador to Russia in 1833 the Tsar refused to receive him. He continued in diplomatic life until his retirement in 1859 when he built Frant Court where he lived until his death at the age of 94 in 1880.

Toilets and refreshments are available in the village.

Public Transport: No direct service from Crowborough. Route 729 operates hourly to Tunbridge Wells (Monday-Saturday) and 2 hourly on Sundays. Route 252 operates hourly to Frant from Tunbridge Wells as does Route 254 although neither operate on a Sunday.

12. Rotherfield

One of the oldest villages in Ashdown Forest; indeed its records are among the oldest in Britain, for it has documents that were in existence before the Norman Conquest. The charm of the village is its church and this too has a story dating back to antiquity, for in the eighth century Berhtwald, Duke of the South Saxons, was a very sick man. Unable to find a cure at home he made a pilgrimage to an abbey in France where the bones of St. Dionysius were said to work miraculous cures. Fulfilling its objective Berhtwald returned cured whereupon he founded the church in 792 AD in honour of St. Denys, although the present church dates back only as far as the thirteenth century.

Inside it houses two great treasures; one, the magnificent pulpit, made by carpenters in the days of Oliver Cromwell and brought from the chapel of the Archbishop of York's palace, while the second was made by carpenters a century earlier and is the superbly carved eight sided font cover, although the font it covers is relatively modern. Wall paintings of extremely good quality are still evident if fading now and almost all the old William Morris stained glass is gone although fragments from Rotherfield's Roman past still remains.

In the churchyard are the remains of Sophia Louisa Jex-Blake who went to the United States in the 1860's to study medicine and surgery and then returned to Britain where she sought to qualify here as a doctor. All the London schools closed their doors to her, but at first Edinburgh relented before it too withdrew its privilege, leaving Miss Jex-Blake with no alternative but to open the London School of Medicine for Women. Within three years the Royal Free Hospital admitted her students to practice and her endeavours had not gone unnoticed in Parliament. In 1876 an act was passed enabling all medical examining bodies to include women candidates and the following year she was able to put up a sign as the first lady doctor in Britain. She lived her last twelve years of an eventful life in Rotherfield where she died in 1912.

Toilets and refreshment facilities available in the village.

Public Transport: Route 226 operated by RDH Services provides a direct link with Crowborough.
Route 729 to Tunbridge Wells connecting with Route 252 to Rotherfield operates a more frequent service. Check times before travelling.

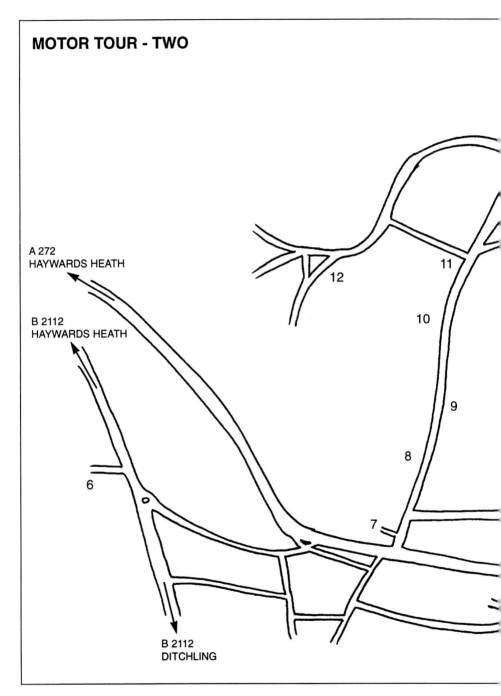

MOTOR TOUR - TWO

A 272
HAYWARDS HEATH

B 2112
HAYWARDS HEATH

12

11

10

9

8

7

6

B 2112
DITCHLING

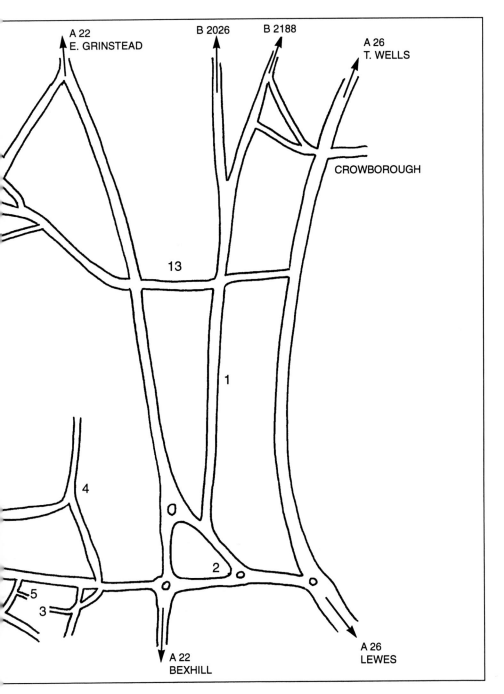

MOTOR TOUR — TWO (48MILE/78.3KM)

CROWBOROUGH — FAIRWARP — MARESFIELD —
BARKHAM MANOR VINEYARDS — FLETCHING —
NEWICK — WIVELSFIELD — CHAILEY — SHEFFIELD PARK
STATION (BLUEBELL RAILWAY) — SHEFFIELD PARK
GARDENS — HEAVEN FARM — DANEHILL — HORSTED .
KEYNES — NUTLEY (WINDMILL) — CROWBOROUGH

1. Crowborough to Fairwarp (6.75mile/11km)

Leave the crossroads westward taking the first left signposted Horder
Centre for Arthritis *and in 2mile (3.3km) turn left onto the B2188
signposted Maresfield. In a further 2.5mile (4.3km) reach Kings Standing
car park on the left as the B2026 merges in from the right and in a further
2.25mile (3.6km) reach Fairwarp church car park on the left.*

*Toilets and refreshment facilities available at Foresters Arms (large
garden/children's play area) in Fairwarp village next left off B2026.*

2. Fairwarp to Maresfield (2mile/3.2km)

*Turn left out of car park and in lmile (1.6km) left again onto A22 into
Maresfield. Turn right at roundbout onto the A272 where there is parking
on the right opposite the church.*

Toilets and refreshment facilities available at Chequers public house.

3. Maresfield to Barkham Manor Vineyards (2.5mile/4km)

*Continue along A272 signposted Haywards Heath and in 2mile (3.3km)
turn left at the second crossroads signposted Shortbridge/Barkham Manor.
Turn right and right again at signs for Barkham Manor through the gates
and along an impressive tree-lined drive to the Vineyards.*

Toilets and refreshment facilities available here.

4. Barkham Manor Vineyards to Fletching (2mile/3.2km)

*Return to crossroads at the A272 crossing straight over signposted
Fletching. Follow the road round right through the village to a car park off
right behind the church.*

Toilets and refreshment facilities available in the village

5. Fletching to Newick (3mile/4.8km)

Left out of car park and past church to bear right at Mill Lane signposted

Newick/Chailey and in 1.75mile (2.8km) turn left again. Turn left onto the A272 and in 200 yards (185m) bear right at the Bull public house. In 0.5mile(0.8km) turn left for the church where limited parking is available. Toilets and refreshment facilities available in the village.

6. Newick to Wivelsfield (10mile/16km)

Left out of church close, turning right then left at staggered crossroads signposted Cooksbridge/Lewes. Continue to A275 at South Chailey where turn left and in 0.75mile (1.2km) right into Mill Lane and right again at T-junction signposted Wivelsfield Green. In a further 1mile (1.6km) turn left signposted Burgess Hill (just past the Plough public house). At the B2112 turn right signposted Wivelsfield and in a further 2mile (3.2km) turn left for Wivelsfield church and the car park off left.
Toilets and refreshments not available here.

7. Wivelsfield to Chailey (4.5mile/7.2km)

Right out of car park and right again at B2112. Bear left at roundabout signposted Wivelsfield Green and in 3mile (4.8km) keep ahead at crossroads turning right onto A272 a few yards further on. In 0.75mile (1.2km) turn left onto the A275 signposted Sheffield Park/East Grinstead, turning left again in 0.25 mile (0.4km) at Warrs Hill signposted New Heritage. In 0.5mile (0.8km) turn left into Red House Common car park.
Toilets and refreshment facilities not available here

8. Chailey to Sheffield Park Station (Bluebell Railway) (1.5mile/2.3km)

Return to A275 and turn left. In little over 1.5mile (2.3km) turn left into Sheffield Park station car park.
Toilets and refreshments available here.

9. Sheffield Park Station to Sheffield Park Gardens (0.5mile/0.8km)

Left onto A275 then right in about 0.5mile (0.8km) for Sheffield Park Gardens.
Toilets and refreshments available here.

10. Sheffield Park Gardens to Heaven Farm (1.5mile/2.3km)

Return to A275 and turn right. In about 1.5mile (2.3km) turn left into Heaven Farm.
Toilets and refreshments available here

11. Heaven Farm to Danehill (1mile/1.6km)

Left onto the A275 and in 0.25mile (0.4km) left again along Church Lane into Danehill where there is limited parking by the church.
Toilets and refreshment facilities not available here.

12. Danehill to Horsted Keynes (1.5mile/2.3km)

Continue downhill to the crossroads, turning left signposted Horsted Keynes, then left again at the T-junction into Horsted Keynes. Parking is available on the left by the Royal British Legion and the playing fields.
Toilets and refreshments available here.

13. Horsted Keynes to Nutley (Windmill) (7.5mile/12km)

Retrace route out of Horsted Keynes keeping ahead in 0.5mile (0.8km) signposted Birch Grove. Follow the road round right past Birch Grove House to the A275 where turn right opposite the Red Lion public house, Chelwood Gate, then left at the staggered crossroads signposted Nutley. In a further 2.5mile (4km) turn sharp left onto the A22 then right signposted Crowborough and 1mile (1.6km) further on is Friends car park on the left.
Toilets and refreshments not available here.

14. Nutley (Windmill) to Crowborough (4.75mile/7.6km)

Continue along the road for 1mile (1.6km) before crossing at the staggered crossroads at the B2026. In 1mile (1.6km) join the A26 to conclude the tour in Crowborough.

POINTS OF INTEREST DURING THE TOUR

1. Fairwarp

There were ironworks here from Roman times, then charcoal-burning, then nursery gardening and even hop growing on land reclaimed from the forest that once enjoyed boom days.

Here too is a ford; a rarity these days and one which the village is proud of, so much so, that when East Sussex County Council channelled the water to run under the road there was such an outcry from the locals that the council workmen had to return to restore the stream to its original course across the lane.

Toilets and refreshment facilities available at the Foresters Arms public house in the village.

Public Transport: There is no suitable public transport passing Fairwarp church

Walk: A splendid walk (6.5mile/10.7km) incorporating much of the forest terrain and visiting Nutley Windmill and the Airman's Grave. (See page 62.)

Fairwarp Church

2. Maresfield

Though only a small village the parish of Maresfield is enormous, encompassing much of the Ashdown Forest. It is of little significance today but it once boasted three ironworks, though there is nothing to recall those far off days save for the hammerponds, some of which are still in evidence.

Maresfield Park, long since gone, is still remembered by the impressive pointed Gothic turret of the lodge marking the entrance now to nowhere. Opposite is the thirteenth century church with splendid timbers and a window painted in memory of poet John Shelley by his daughter Blanche.

Toilets and refreshment facilities available at the Chequers public house on the roundabout.

Public Transport: There is no direct public transport from Crowborough. Route 729 operates an hourly service to Uckfield where Route 781 connects with an hourly service to Maresfield (weekdays only). On Saturdays there is a 2hourly service with no service on Sundays.
Walk: An 8.5mile (14km) walk starts from here passing the old iron industry hammerponds, Piltdown golf course and the entrance to Barkham Manor vineyards. The return route visits the pretty village of Fletching. (See page 67.)

3. Barkham Manor Vineyards

Mentioned in Domesday Book, Barkham Manor was given to Earl Goodwin by King Edward when it was valued at 20 shillings. In 1409 it was held by Thomas Skelton and his wife Johan. In 1723 it passed to Thomas Maryon-Wilson whose family held the titles of Lords of Netherhall, Barkham and Tarring Chamois. By the mid 1830's the Maryon-Wilsons had demolished the earlier house replacing it with the majority of the present house on the same site. This was extended by the Kerr family in the 1920's to create the well proportioned Manor of today.

The famous vineyards were planted in 1985 and grows six varieties of wine; German Huxelrebe, Bacchus, Muller Thurgau, Kerner, Schonburger and the French Pinot Noir ranging from dry to medium sweet in a variety of styles to suit all palates. Apart from home consumption they are also exported to places as diverse as Japan, France, Germany and Taiwan.

Because of the variance in climatic conditions with frequent spring frosts, a high trellis system known as Geneva Double Curtain (GDC) has been developed to protect the young grapes from inclement weather. Harvesting usually takes place in mid-October with fermentation taking place during the winter producing wine ready to drink in the spring.

Apart from guided tours of the winery, facilities also include a shop offering wine tasting and subservient products. The Great Thatched Barn, dating from 1750 and now beautifully restored, is frequently used for Art Exhibitions and Antiques Fairs as well as for Wedding Receptions and Private Functions. A vineyard trail explains more about the variety of grapes and the wines they produce and there is also a picnic area and adequate car parking.

Toilets and picnic facilities available.

Piltdown Man

In 1911, Charles Dawson, a lawyer and amateur archaeologist, claimed to have found the fossilised fragments of pieces of skull and jaw bone in the vicinity of the vineyards. On 18th December 1912 the discovery was announced by Dawson and Sir Arthur Smith Woodward, of the Natural History department of the British Museum, to the Geological Society of London and the missing link in man's evolution from apes was believed to have been found. Pieces of skull and jaw bone enabled scientists to reconstruct the skull of what was to be known as the Piltdown Skull. Subsequent finds in the area won over most of the remaining sceptics and these *remains* are still on view in the Natural History Museum in London. But in 1949, Dr K.P. Oakley applied the modern flourine dating test to Piltdown Man and one of the greatest hoaxes in history became evident. Chemical and physical evidence based on carbon dating indicated the fragments dated between AD1000 and 1900 and in no way could be part of man's ancestry. To this day the identity and motives of the hoaxer(s) remain a mystery.

Opening Times: 10am-5pm Tuesday-Sunday and Bank Holidays Tel: 01825 722103

Public Transport: There is no direct public transport from Crowborough. Route 729 operates an hourly service to Uckfield where Route 246 (operated by RDH Services) sets down at Piltdown Crossroads (necessitating approx 1 mile (1.6km) walk to Barkham Manor) once a day (Mondays and Fridays only). The return service allows about two and a half hours before picking up at the same crossroads. Confirm times of connections before travelling.

4. Fletching

There is no mention in Domesday Book, but a stone church was built thereabouts for there are traces of late Saxon or early Norman work in the tower of the present building which was completed around 1230. It was confirmed to the Priory of Michelham in 1398 by the Bishop of Chichester and at the Dissolution of the Monasteries the patronage was granted to Anne of Cleves, afterwards passing to the Dorset family from whom it was purchased by the first Earl of Sheffield. It remained with the successive owners of Sheffield Park until 1956 when it passed into the hands of the Archbishop of Canterbury.

One of the church's quaintest possessions is a brass in the south transept mounted upon a stone slab. Quite unique of its kind it is dedicated to Peter Denot and indicates his vocation as a glover and is dated around 1450. Along with other Fletching men he took part in Jack Cade's Rebellion for which he was subsequently pardoned. Another brass is a memorial to a member of the Dalyngrygge family depicting a knight in full armour alongside his lady. This was the family which built Bodiam Castle and the family crest of the unicorn's head is over the castle gate.

Two famous names from history are also associated with the church. In 1264 Simon de Montfort, on the eve of the Battle of Lewes, came with his barons to pray and to receive the Holy Sacrament with the Bishop of Worcester celebrating. Legend has it that a number of de Montfort's knights who were slain the next day were carried back to Fletching and hurriedly buried in full armour beneath the nave of the church. The Battle of Lewes won led to the calling of a Parliament in which the birth of the House of Commons could have been conceived.

The other name is that of the famous historian, Edward Gibbon, author of *The Decline and Fall of the Roman Empire.* He was a great friend of the first Earl of Sheffield and was buried in the Sheffield Mausoleum in January 1794.

Toilets and refreshments available in the village.

Back entrance to Sheffield Park, Fletching

Fletching village

Public Transport: There is no direct public transport from Crowborough. Route 729 operates an hourly service to Uckfield where Route 246 (operated by RDH Services) connects with a single bus on Mondays and Fridays only allowing approx. two and a quarter hours stay in the village before the only return back to Uckfield. Check on times of buses before travelling.

5. Newick

This pretty little village is clustered around a triangular green complete with parish pump, which was erected by local plumber Richard Fuller over a well sunk by Arthur and Jack Wood to commemorate Queen Victoria's Diamond Jubilee celebrations in 1897. In those days Newick was pretty well self sufficient and has absorbed a massive population boom since the Second World War.

Its church lies a little way back from the green and boasts a Jacobean pulpit and stained glass dating from 1315. Unfortunately it is kept locked so the ironwork on the cover of the fourteenth century font cannot be appreciated, nor the dignified reredos; or the altar-work made by a friend of the church who never attended it, for her ten years toil of love was done in bed.

The old turnpike toll house still stands beside the A272 and Blind Lane

Newick village sign

may well be so called from the toll dodgers who used it as a bypass well out of sight of the toll house, to avoid payments which could be fairly hefty.

The village has connections with several distinguished names from the past. In the 1920's the cricketing brothers James and John Langridge began their careers on the village cricket pitch, both going on to play for Sussex and James for England. James was the bowler and his brother a batsman and shrewd slip fielder. Together they became a formidable combination for the entry *"caught Langridge (John) bowled Langridge (James)"* occurs 133 times in the score books. Among those who encouraged the two brothers to develop their skills was Thomas Baden Powell, cousin of Lord Baden Powell, founder of the Scout movement.

Playing the lead in the Newick Amateur Dramatic Society 1934 production of *Journey's End* was Derek Bogaerde. It was his first major stage part but he went on to achieve world fame on the silver screen as matinee idol Dirk Bogarde.

Toilets and refreshments available at a choice of venues in the village.

Public Transport: There is no direct service from Crowborough. Route 729 operates an hourly service to Uckfield where Route 781 connects with an hourly service to Newick (2-hourly on Saturdays) with no service on Sundays.

Wivelsfield Church

6. Wivelsfield

Wifelesfelde — meaning quite simply Wifel's field - was mentioned as early as AD765 in an Anglo-Saxon Charter, suggesting that here was a clearing in the Weald or forest that was prevalent in this part of Sussex.

The single street that accommodates some lovely old houses, the church and village school, has two charming eighteenth century houses at either end; More House to the east and Lunces Hall to the west. The former was originally built for the oldest family in Wivelsfield, soldiers from their earliest days until their extinction; both are now farmhouses.

No toilets or refreshments available here.

Public Transport: No public transport passes Wivelsfield with easy access from Crowborough.

Walk: A very pleasant 4.25mile (7km) walk through some lovely Wealdland countryside offering a shortened version of 3miles (4.8km) if preferred. (See page 70.)

7. Chailey

Its name is descriptive of its locality for since Anglo-Saxon times *Chag* meant gorse and *ley* was an open space or meadow, hence *Chagley* was an open space covered in gorse.

The earliest mention of the place is in two charters of the eleventh century and it was not until the mid sixteenth century that it was pronounced *Chalaghe*.

It is one of the largest villages in England, covering a border of 24 mile, although to be more precise it is three communities in one; North Chailey, South Chailey and Chailey Green, the latter being the original community developing around the church. In modern times all development took place north and south of the parish and in due course conditions in the Green changed and the shops and other activities have all moved to the busier areas.

No toilets or refreshments available here.

Public Transport: No direct service from Crowborough. Route 729 operates an hourly service to Uckfield where Route 781 connects with an hourly service to North Chailey (King's Head crossroads) (2-hourly on Saturdays) with no service on Sundays. (N.B. Red House Common car park is 0.75mile (1.2km) walk from the crossroads following Motor Tour -Two route directions — see page 31).

Walk: An 8mile (12.8km) circuit including the most interesting features of this fascinating part of Sussex. (See page 75.)

8. Sheffield Park Station (Bluebell Railway)

In 1876 the Lewes & East Grinstead Railway was formed by a group of local landowners as a means of transporting products to and from their estates. The Chairman was the Earl of Sheffield, whose estate was at Sheffield Park, but even he and his wealthy backers soon realised the funding of such a project as the L&EGR was even beyond their pockets. So they sought help from existing railway companies and in 1878 approached the London, Brighton & South Coast Railway, who were most anxious to keep their close rival the South Eastern Railway from gaining a foothold in their territory and thus having access to the lucrative traffic to Brighton and Eastbourne. The LBSCR saw the L&EGR's request for help as the ideal opportunity to thwart South Eastern's plans for a railway through Beckenham to East Grinstead then on to Brighton, that they agreed to meet the debts in land aquisition, construct the line and operate it. The Lewes — East Grinstead line opened on 1st August 1882 and once it became operational the L&EGR passed into oblivion with the line becoming part of the LBSCR system. Soon the Lewes & East Grinstead Railway was forgotten but it was to prove of vital importance almost three-quarters of a century later.

'Stepney' — Bluebell Railway

The Railway prospered right up until after the First World War when the motor lorry began to take away lucrative parts of their staple goods traffic. The motor bus took even more income away during the 1930's and by the time the railways were nationalised in 1948 the Railway's traffic had dwindled to practically nothing. Somehow it managed to survive until the line was closed on 28th May 1955 without ceremony. Then a local resident discovered the closure was in fact illegal; for the original Act of Parliament, transferring operation of the line from the L&EGR to the LBSCR, required the latter to run at least four trains a day, stopping at specified stations, in return for taking over the L&EGR's assets. Although these commitments had subsequently passed to British Railways on nationalisation, they were compelled by law to reopen the line and run the statutory four trains a day, which they did, pending a further Act of Parliament relinquishing their obligations. Naturally the line became a political issue and the press had a field day, christening the Railway the Bluebell Line which achieved national acclaim by the time final closure was secured on 16th March 1958.

A year later the Lewes &East Grinstead Railway Preservation Society was formed and the Bluebell Railway opened in 1960 as the first standard guage passenger carrying preserved railway. Because British Railways still operated tracks to the goods yard at Horsted Keynes they would not allow the Bluebell

'Giants of Steam' — Bluebell Railway

Railway to use Horsted Keynes station, so instead a halt had to be constructed on the single track just outside the station limits. This necessitated a second locomotive to work the return journey as there was no means of transferring a locomotive from one end of the train to the other. Late in 1961 they were able to operate into Horsted Keynes station and two years later British Railways relinquished their services to the station and the Bluebell Railway had sole rights to its usage. In April 1994 the much sought after extension of the Line to Kingscote was opened for passenger traffic and the final stretch to East Grinstead was within sight. Planning permission for such a project has already been given and the Bluebell Railway has until February 2001 to complete the ambition of operating into East Grinstead adjacent to Network SouthCentral's terminus.

Run almost entirely by volunteers the cost of operating the railway and the restoration and maintenance of its collection of historic items comes from fares and sales and donations. Today it is world famous attracting over 200,000 visitors a year.

Toilets and refreshments available here.

Times of Opening: See timetable published annually from all information bureaus or telephone - 01825 722370.

Public Transport: There is no direct public transport from Crowborough. Route 729 operates an hourly service to Uckfield where Route 246 (operated by RDH Services) connects with a single bus on Mondays and Fridays, only allowing approx. two and a half hours stay before the only return back to Uckfield. Check on times of buses before travelling.

9. Sheffield Park Gardens

The name *Sheffield* appears in Domesday Book when it meant *sheep clearing* which would suggest that this well-wooded part of Sussex had been open country since Saxon times. Sheffield Park, originally known as Sheffield Place, is an ancient estate belonging to King Harold's father, Godwin, Earl of Kent. After the Norman Conquest it was given by William to his half brother Robert de Mortain, Earl of Cornwall. By 1264 the estate belonged to Simon de Montfort, who camped his rebel army at nearby Fletching before defeating Henry III at the Battle of Lewes. From 1292 the estate was in the hands of the Lords de la Warr until falling in to the hands of Sir Edward Dalyngrigge in the 1380's. Sir Edward became even more famous as the builder of Bodiam Castle. In 1444 it was seized by Henry VI before passing onto Thomas Howard, 3rd Duke of Norfolk, who entertained Henry VIII here in August 1538. There then followed a period when the estate belonged to the Earls of Bergavenny (latterly Abergavenney) then the Sackvilles of Knole before belonging to the Nevilles in 1623. It reverted back to the de la Warrs in the early eighteenth century who were responsible for much of the earlier planning of the current landscaping by planting long avenues of oak and ash running northwards from the old

Sheffield Park Gardens (National Trust)

Sheffield Park (the house is not open to the public)

mansion, which occupied the same site as the current house. Running east they planted rows of chestnut, walnut and cherry and between 1745 and 1769 created a lake from what had been no more than a stream.

In 1769 John Baker Holroyd purchased the estate and was created the 1st Earl of Sheffield in 1816. He extended the work in transforming the grounds, employing the services of 'Capability' Brown at one time, although there is little or no evidence today of what the great man achieved. Under the 2nd Earl, who succeeded his father in 1821, the park stood somewhat neglected but achieved a remarkable revival under the 3rd Earl whose first love was cricket. With the aid of his gardener, William Thomas Moore, the 3rd Earl laid out the basic skeleton of the planting seen today. In 1885 he began an arboretum consisting of exotic and native trees and much of the artificial waterfalls and water terraces were commissioned by him. His latter years were clouded with disputes with the neighbours and he spent long periods in France where he died in 1909, leaving no heir and a debt-ridden estate.

Arthur Gilstrap Soames, a wealthy Lincolnshire brewer, purchased the estate in 1910 and almost at once began planting on an enormous scale. The rhododendrons were introduced by him for which Sheffield Park is nowadays so well known, indeed much of what we see today was the creation of Arthur Soames, who married late in life and died in 1934. His widow stayed on as tenant right through the Second World War until finally giving up Sheffield Park to her nephew who restored the gardens to their pre-war condition before being obliged to sell in 1953. In 1954 Sheffield Park Gardens were acquired by the National Trust who did much to restore them to their former glory, hampered only by the Great Storm

of 1987. Today they are back to their best with a series of walks and paths through and around a series of lakes and ponds begun 250 years ago by the prodigious de la Warrs.
Toilets and refreshement facilities available.

Opening Times: March, weekends only 11-6; April-November, daily (except Mondays) 11-6 or sunset if earlier (Bank Holidays included); December, daily (except Mondays and Tuesdays) 11-4

Public Transport: There is no direct public transport from Crowborough. Route 729 operates an hourly service to Uckfield where Route 246 (operated by RDH Services) connects with a single bus on Mondays and Fridays only, allowing two and a half hours stay before the only return back to Uckfield. Check on times of buses before travelling

10. Heaven Farm

The history of Heaven Farm is well documented back as far as 1387 although the present farm buildings originate from about 170 years ago. The buildings, which include barn, stables, slaughterhouse, granary, worksheds, piggeries, forge and oast house enabled a remarkable range of farming activities to be carried out and are preserved as a museum with their original contents.

By contrast a new farm, built in 1964, is also available to view showing the most up-to-date farming techniques associated with cows and cereals.

A lovely nature trail through ancient woodland is an absolute delight in spring with its bluebells and enenomes and there is a craft shop and tea rooms to satisfy every visitors needs.

Toilets and refreshment facilities available.

Opening Times: March-October 10.30am - 6pm

Public Transport: Heaven Farm is not served by public transport

11. Danehill

Although Neolithic stone age flints, iron age pottery and Roman iron smelting sites have all been found in the area, no Saxon remains have been discovered, which seems strange since the village is apparently named from their era, being derived from the word *Denn*, meaning a woodland pig pasture.

The first known reference to the village is dated 1265 although the earliest existing building belongs to the early fifteenth century. All Saints Church replaced the first church to be built in Danehill which occupied the site where the War Memorial now stands. It was seriously damaged by fire

Danehurst (now St. Raphael's Nursing Home).

and although repaired by Mr Herbert Hardy of nearby Danehurst, the insurance money was to help pay for a new church in due course. The following year Mr Hardy died as a result of an accident and his widow offered the money to build the new church in his memory. The foundation stone was laid on All Saints Day 1891 and work on the new church proceeded rapidly. It was consecrated on 12th August 1892 and built of Wealden sandstone in the Decorated and Perpendicular style with Collyweston slate roof.

Danehurst, the home of Herbert C. Hardy, was built in the 1820's by Col. Francis Davies and bought by Mr Hardy in 1875, whose family continued to live on there following his untimely death in 1888. It was bought by Mr G.D. Haslam who, as a churchwarden from 1929-45, was very involved in church affairs. It is now St Raphael's Nursing Home and remains an imposing looking building to this day.

There are no public toilets or refreshment facilities available here.

Public Transport: Danehill is not easily accessible by public transport from Crowborough.

12. Horsted Keynes

There was an ancient settlement here long before the church was built and it is firmly believed it stands on the site of a pagan temple, which was often the practice a thousand years ago. If this be true then it would explain why the church's orientation is not east to west as normal but nearer north-east to south-west — very similar to Stonehenge — to receive the rays of the rising sun at the Summer solstice.

The Saxon village would have been situated next to the church which has some stonework in the tower and a doorway of Saxon date. The Saxon name for the village was *Horsted*, a place where horses are kept.

The Normans took the manor following the Conquest in 1066 and it then belonged to Ralf de Cahaignes, a man with possessions in that part of Normandy. And so the village became known as *Horsted de Cahaignes* (pronounced Canes) and over the years gradually became known as Horsted Keynes.

Toilets and refreshments available in the village.

Public Transport: Horsted Keynes is not easily accessible by public transport from Crowborough.

Walk: A majestic outing starting out along the Sussex Border path, skirkting the attractive hammerponds before passing Broadhurst Manor and its animal sanctuary then returning alongside the Bluebell Line and Horsted Keynes station before the picturesque return to St Giles Church and its interesting churchyard. (See page 80.)

13. Nutley (Windmill)

Thought to have been brought here from Goudhurst in Kent, it is perhaps genuinely the oldest post-mill standing in Sussex today. There is no record of the mill standing here before 1840 although inside is the inscription WS 1817. Records show that the mill finished working around 1908 and the structure of the body had failed during the latter years of its working life. It is an open trestle mill and until 1971 was shored up on steel joists and brick piers, which its owner Lady Castle-Stuart had placed to save the mill from collapse during an early renovation in 1928. By 1972 the mill was working again for the first time in 64 years due to a complete restoration when the

Nutley post-mill

weatherboarding was completely renewed. The work gained an Architectural Heritage Year Award in 1975 and was carried out by the Nutley Preservation Society, bringing the mill from near collapse in 1969 to the almost perfect condition seen today. As mills go it is rather small, standing only fifteen feet from head to tail and just ten feet wide. The centre post is very old and is studded with hundreds of nails, perhaps to prevent the splintered grain snagging the miller's clothing. The windshaft is of iron and is nineteenth century.

There are no toilets or refreshment facilities available here.

Opening Times: Open the last Sunday of each month from June-September inclusive between 2.30 and 5.30pm

Public Transport: Nutley Windmill is not served by any public transport

Walk: Walk 4 may start from Friends car park and the directions followed from point four (4).

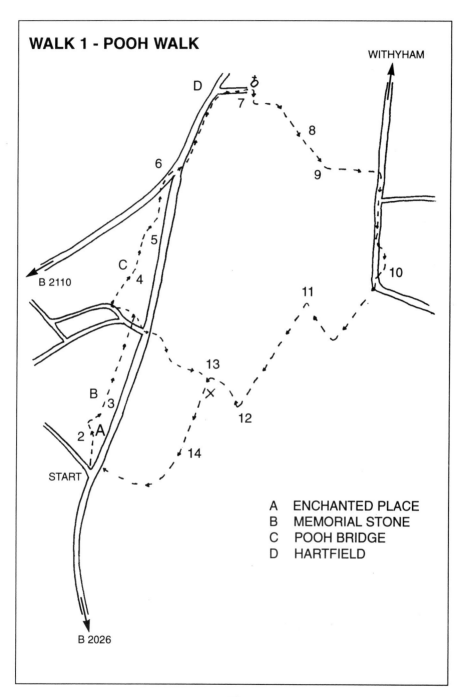

WALK 1 - POOH WALK

WITHYHAM

D

7

8

9

6

5

C

4

B 2110

10

11

13

B

3

X

12

2 A

14

START

A   ENCHANTED PLACE
B   MEMORIAL STONE
C   POOH BRIDGE
D   HARTFIELD

B 2026

WALK 1 — POOH WALK

Access/Parking:	Gills Lap car park at the junction of the B2026 Hartfield road and a minor road to Colemans Hatch
Map Reference:	Landranger 188 grid reference 468315
Distance:	8.5 miles (14km) or 5 miles (8km)
Time to Allow:	4.5 hours or 2.5 hours
Terrain:	Easy walking along forest rides and paths and metalled road
Toilets/Refreshments:	In Hartfield. (None on shortened version)
Route:	Gills Lap-Enchanted Place-Lone Pine-Memorial Stone-Pooh Bridge-Pooh Corner-Hartfield-Fishers Gate-North Pole-Five Hundred Acre Wood-Gills Lap

Still a very pleasant walk even if not a Pooh fan, along an undulating fire ride and through pleasant woods to Pooh Bridge. Here the main walk carries on into Hartfield then back along a country lane to Fishers Gate where the route re-enters the forest and along the Wealdway back to Gills Lap. The shortened version retraces its steps back from Pooh Bridge to rejoin the main route on the outskirts of Five Hundred Acre Wood back to the car park.

Directions:

1. *Head east along a fire ride running parallel with the B2026 to a trig point on the right next to which is the Enchanted Place* **(A)**
2. *Return to the main ride which cross straight over along a well defined footpath to the Lone Pine. Opposite the Lone Pine turn right and right again at the main track, taking a path off left in 20 yards (16m) to the Memorial Stone* **(B)**
3. *Turn left at the original fire ride, keeping slightly to the right of the house before crossing the road and into the woods, emerging again at a road by Andbell House. Keep straight ahead along the road and in 30 yards (24m) turn right at the public footpath sign to Pooh Bridge* **(C)**
4. *To continue with the main route, cross the bridge to join a metalled drive, keeping ahead (ignoring the right turn) and where the drive veers left keep ahead over the stile beside a gate following an obvious path across two fields with a stile between them.***(see point 13)*
5. *In the top right corner of the second field cross a stile, proceeding right for a few paces before crossing another stile and keeping to the hedge on the left along the next field, from which there are extensive views to*

the right across Ashdown Forest. Over another stile and turn left, then across another stile in a few paces following the left edge of two fields, when the spire of Hartfield church is evident to the right.

6. Turn right at the B2110 into Hartfield **(D)** passing Pooh Corner with its Pooh memorabilia and turning right at the Anchor Inn to Hartfield Church.

7. Opposite the church turn right up the steps and over a stile before turning left along the edge of two fields. At the third field keep ahead (ignoring the well trodden path left) passing to the right of a row of trees.

8. In the bottom field corner cross the stile beside a gate, continuing ahead to a metal gate, keeping alongside the left edge of the next field past the house on the left.

9. Cross the bridge before turning left past a rustic bridge (which do not cross), to continue along a green track beyond a stile and across a field, to join a drive onto which turn right and follow for a mile (1.6km) to Fishers Gate, passing Buckhurst Manor on the right.

10. After the diversion rejoin the drive and fork right, forking right again at the next two junctions, dropping down past a house and garden surrounded by a high fence.

11. At the top of the next rise turn left, following the Wealdway signs as the track climbs for over a mile (1.6km), marked at first by yellow arrows and then through Five Hundred Acre Wood by wooden posts.

12. At the second wooden post turn sharp right along a well defined path which soon spreads out to be a much wider track, where a caravan site is evident on the slope opposite. Turn left at the T-junction (point X)

13. *To proceed with the shortened version of the walk, retrace steps back to the road where turn left past Andbells and into the woods. Take the left fork through the wooden chicane to Pooh car park and out on to the road where turn left as far as the B2026. Cross straight over road and into woods, turning right in front of three large houses, crossing a gravel track and continuing ahead along a narrow track which eventually merges into a much wider track. Keep ahead over a stream and up to a wide fire ride where turn right to reach point X on the main route.

14. Follow this wide ride round right past "Eeyor's sad and gloomy place" back to Gills Lap to conclude the walk.

POINTS OF INTEREST ON THE WALK

(A) Enchanted Place

Christoper Robin called this clump the Enchanted Place because nobody

Pooh Bridge

had ever been able to determine whether it was 63 or 64 trees in the circle. Also he was able to sit down carelessly here without getting prickled, unlike anywhere else in the Forest.

(B) Memorial Stone

In an area enclosed by a chestnut paling fence is a large stone bearing a memorial to AA Milne the author and EH Shepard the illustrator of the Winnie the Pooh books.

(C) Pooh Bridge

Built in 1907 by JC Osman it was restored in 1979 by the National Westminster Bank and DLS Ltd. for East Sussex County Council. It was here in the books the game of Pooh sticks was played and few who visit this magical place can resist tossing a twig in the stream below.

(D) Hartfield see page 20.

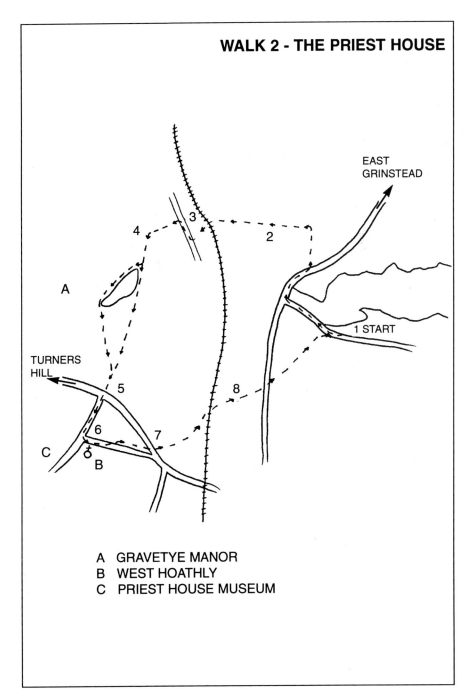

WALK 2 - THE PRIEST HOUSE

EAST
GRINSTEAD

3

4

2

A

1 START

TURNERS
HILL

5

8

6

7

C

B

A GRAVETYE MANOR
B WEST HOATHLY
C PRIEST HOUSE MUSEUM

WALK 2 — THE PRIEST HOUSE

Access/Parking: Weir Wood Reservoir car park
Map Reference: Landranger 187 grid reference 383341
Distance: 6 miles (10km)
Time to Allow: 3 hours
Terrain: Initial scramble over rocks before following well defined paths, tracks and metalled roads over an easy course
Toilets/Refreshments: Cat Inn, West Hoathly; Vinols Cross Inn and Bluebell Inn en route
Route: Weir Wood Reservoir-Gravetye Lower Lake-Gravetye Manor-West Hoathly Church-Priest House-Bluebell Inn and Railway-New Coombe Farm-Sussex Border Path-Neylands Farm-Weir Wood Reservoir

An easy walk, initially with good views overlooking Weir Wood Reservoir before crossing the Bluebell Railway and reaching Gravetye Lower Lake, where there is a choice of routes. A deep, enclosed track leads into the village of West Hoathly with its interesting church and nearby Priest House Museum and the return route skirts the Bluebell Line once again (with excellent views of the trains if operating) before cutting back through the playing fields and Neylands Farm to the Reservoir car park.

Directions:

1. *Turn right out of the car park to T-junction, where turn right again then left by the East Grinstead sign. Over stile, keeping ahead to rocks, which clamber up to footpath above, where turn left.*

2. *Through the gate to an open field which continue ahead across in the direction of the public footpath sign towards the pylon. Cross the bridge and turn left, following the path up and over the railway to a metalled road where turn right.*

3. *In the bottom of the dip turn left over a stile immediately past a bridge over a stream. Cross the field and enter the woods, crossing the main track and continuing through a metal kissing gate.*

4. *Turn left at the public footpath sign once again into the woods. (This stretch could be very muddy after wet weather!) On the right is Gravetye Lower Lake and a choice of route. For good views of Gravetye Manor (A) keep alongside the hedge on the right, crossing the stone stile before crossing the next field diagonally right, heading to a point right of a small copse ahead. At the public footpath signpost (where there*

are good views of the Manor to the right) turn left and over another stile before bearing right onto a deep track which follow to the road.
To walk by the lake, enter the enclosure taking the path round to the right of the lake. To circumnavigate the lake, take the first turning left at the far end of the lake, to return to the small gate then continue the walk as described. By taking the second turning left at the far end of the lake then right at the public footpath, continue through the squeeze stile into the woods following the signs for High Weald Landscape Trail. The trail eventually leads into the same deep track as above which follow to the road.

5. *Cross straight over into North Lane as far as West Hoathly church (B) with Priest House Museum (C) opposite.*

6. *Turn left at the church then left again a little further along, up the steps to a footpath above the road where turn right as far as the crossroads by Vinols Cross Inn.*

7. *Cross the road and continue down a track as far as the Bluebell Inn, continuing along the Sussex Border Path, which is now a concrete road leading to New Coombe Farm. Pass under the railway, following signs for the Border Path.*

8. *As the concrete road swings off left, keep straight ahead along a well defined path across the field by the treatment works. Follow an enclosed path through the playing fields as far as the road, where turn left then right almost immediately past the brick cottage. Keep ahead at the farm buildings before looking for a snicket through right down to the road. Turn right at the road back to the car park*

POINTS OF INTEREST ON THE WALK

(A) Gravetye Manor

A beautiful Elizabethan manor with great brick chimneys, Gravetye was built in 1598 by the local iron-master Richard Infield on a hill and overlooking a lake from which the mighty Medway springs. Its glory is its gardens created by William Robertson who was born in Ireland in 1838 and who rose from garden boy to foreman in Ballykilcannon. He left Ireland in 1861 for the Royal Botanic Society's gardens in Regents Park where he prospered, educated himself and became the gardening correspondent of the *Times* when he founded several gardening journals. He was able to afford to buy Gravetye in 1884 when he created the beautiful gardens there until his death at 97 in 1935. He is still renowned as one of England's greatest gardeners for his imaginative approach to landscape gardening; romantic, naturalistic, never formal with his *wild* gardens of informal planting of rare trees and flowers against a backdrop of parkland, woods and rocky outcrop.

The manor is now an exclusive hotel but as William Robertson decreed in his will, the gardens are open for all to see and enjoy.

(B)   West Hoathly

Nestling on a ridge at the edge of Ashdown Forest West Hoathly is an ancient village full of charm and beauty with the church of St Margaret its crowning glory. The unique churchyard consists of six terraces each built up with a retaining wall and in springtime are a blaze of colour. The church represents many different periods, for the north wall of the nave was built around 1090 and formed part of a small rectangular Norman church. The font was made about 1180 and the big oak chest, hollowed from a single log, may be as old as the thirteenth century and used to collect money for the Crusades. The church was enlarged in the 1200's by building the chancel and the tower was added in the early fifteenth century, which houses six bells, the oldest dating from around 1550. On the wall at the back of the church are the old iron clockworks which used to hang in the tower. By contrast all the stained glass is modern.

(C) Priest House Museum

This early fifteenth century timber-framed farmhouse belonged to Lewes Priory and was most probably a medieval vicarage or estate office and was part of the dowry of Anne of Cleves. In 1524 Lewes Priory leased the Manor of the Rectory of West Hoathly to a John Browne. When he died his son Thomas bought the freehold in 1560. During the prosperous years of Elizabeth I's reign money became available for modificications and im-provements to Old Houses such as the Priest House and chimneys and upper floors were installed. The estate remained in the Browne family until the end of the seventeenth century when financial difficulties forced them to sell. It became neglected, although a subsequent owner did attempt repairs in the middle of the eighteenth century though by 1900 it had become a ruin. In 1905 it was bought by John Godwin King who restored the house, making the north end into a museum, which he opened in 1908. In 1935 it was presented to the Sussex Archaeological Society who restored it as a folk museum of rural life with a delightful collection of furniture, kitchenware, toys and needlework. Upstairs, in the south bedroom, is a sixteenth century wall painting, one of very few Tudor wall paintings still surviving in Sussex today.

Opening Times: Daily 11-5.30 (Sundays 2-5.30) 1st March - 31st October
Admission charge
  Tel: 01342-810479

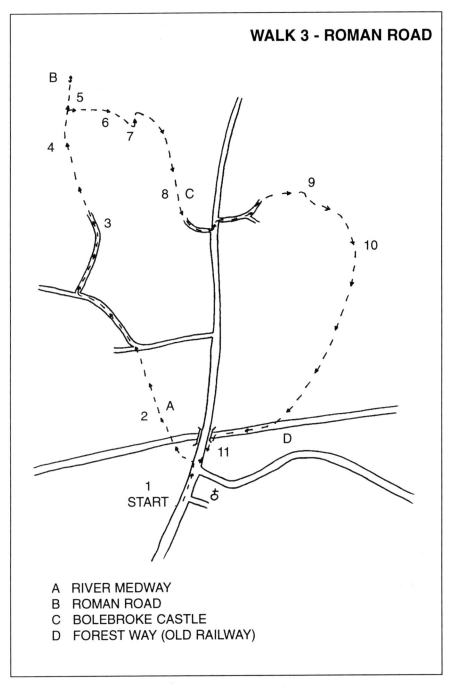

WALK 3 - ROMAN ROAD

A RIVER MEDWAY
B ROMAN ROAD
C BOLEBROKE CASTLE
D FOREST WAY (OLD RAILWAY)

WALK 3 — ROMAN ROAD

Access/Parking: Alongside the road in Hartfield
Map Reference: Landranger 188 grid reference 478356
Distance: 8 miles (12.8km)
Time to Allow: 3 hours
Terrain: Easy walking along woodland tracks, metalled road and disused railway
Toilets/Refreshments: Anchor Inn or the Haywaggon Inn at Hartfield
Route: Hartfield-River Medway-Bassett's Manor-RomanRoad-Chantler's Farm-Bolebroke Castle-Perryhill Farm-River Medway-Forest Way (Dis used railway) Hartfield

A very special walk with plenty of interest beginning with a lovely walk through the woods, before crossing an infant Medway stream en route to the mini industrious Bassett's Manor. The unique stretch of Roman Road is next at Holtye before heading east just a stone's throw south of the Kent border to the woods and Bolebroke Castle. Once through the neat paddocks of Perryhill Farm there is a splendid view overlooking Withyham and Hartfield before dropping down to the disused railway track which leads back to the old station buildings and Hartfield church.

Directions:

1. *Turn left at the public bridleway by October Cottage. Pass through a metal gate before keeping straight ahead over an old railway track then along the lower track as indicated by the blue waymarker.*
2. *Cross the River Medway (A) then through the woods to the road, where keep ahead as far as Yew Tree Cottage where turn right along the public footpath to Bassetts Manor.*
3. *Keep left of the Manor House, passing the stables on the right. Then keep right past the small industrial units to turn left through a metal gate before staying ahead along a concrete track. As the track peters out into pasture, keep ahead passing through two gates in quick succession.*
4. *Take the right fork through the small enclosure turning left opposite the pylon and pass underneath the power lines to the old crosstracks signpost. To visit the Roman Road (B) keep ahead into woods then down next field alongside hedge on right and return.*
5. *At the crosstracks signpost turn right (turn left if returning from Roman Road) taking the left fork under the power lines.*
6. *Through the 5-bar gate on the right near the end of the field, following an obvious path and the yellow waymarkers.*

7. *Cross the stile and turn left at the T-junction, past Chantlers Farm before turning right just past the power lines. Follow the path as far as the public bridleway signpost where turn left into the woods (which are covered in bluebells in the spring.)*
8. *Pass Bolebroke Castle (C) turning left then right to the road. At the road turn left then in 50 yards (45m) turn right along a public bridleway past Perryhill Oast.*
9. *Fork right at the bottom of the hill then left up the edge of the next field and into woods. Cross the stile before bearing right across the next field and through the metal gate.*
10. *Bear right along a wide track with grazing paddock to the right. Keep straight ahead through Top Hill Farm and woods to emerge at a spectacular view over Hartfield to the right. Bear right at the public footpath signpost across the field to merge at the bottom with the Wealdway. Cross the bridge over the river to turn right onto the old railway (D).*
11. *Turn left immediately before the bridge once past the old Hartfield station to return to the village to conclude the walk.*

POINTS OF INTEREST ON THE WALK

(A) River Medway

Hard though it is to imagine, this narrow stream transforms itself into the copious flow of the mighty Medway that 70 miles (112km) upstream joins

River Medway

the Thames at Sheerness to form its estuary with the North Sea. En route on its banks stand Tonbridge, Maidstone, Rochester and Chatham but these are all in Kent. From its source at Gravetye it meanders placidly through Sussex while developing into a navigatable river in Kent and becoming tidal beyond Allington Lock near Maidstone.

(B) Roman Road

This stretch of the London-Lewes way, one of three Roman roads coming down into Sussex from London, was primarily an industrial route. Linking the corn growing area of the South Downs to the capital it also provided outlets for Wealden iron to the ports and naval establishments on the coast. An excavation cleared a hundred yards (90m) of it in 1930 and the grooves cut by the iron tyres of wagons could then be clearly seen. This would have been an early route and iron slag from the foundries along the line of it was used for the metalling. This would have been pounded and watered until it rusted into a solid concrete-like mass. The short stretch on public view is fenced off and is maintained by the Sussex Archaeological Trust.

Roman Road

Forest Way

(C) Bolebroke Castle

Originally a seventeenth century fortified manor house whose original gateway is still standing. Today it is used as a hotel and conference centre but is still impressive with extensive gardens and lake.

(D) Forest Way (Old Railway)

The disused railway from East Grinstead to Groombridge has been designated a Country Park and is accessible on foot, horseback or cycle along its entire length. The platform at Withyam is still in situ and the station buildings at Hartfield have been converted into a private residence and but for the demolition of the bridge across the A22 north of Forest Row is devoid of motor traffic. Along its eastern section are the remains of Brambletye House (see page 18).

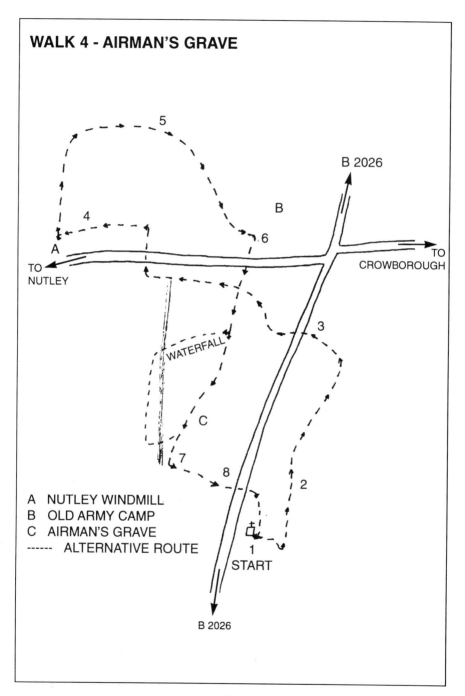

WALK 4 - AIRMAN'S GRAVE

5

B 2026

B

4

A

TO
NUTLEY

TO
CROWBOROUGH

6

WATERFALL

3

C

7

8

2

A   NUTLEY WINDMILL
B   OLD ARMY CAMP
C   AIRMAN'S GRAVE
------   ALTERNATIVE ROUTE

1
START

B 2026

WALK 4 — AIRMAN'S GRAVE

Access/Parking:	Fairwarp church off B2026
Map Reference:	Landranger 188 grid reference 466268
Distance:	6.5 miles (10.7km)
Time to Allow:	2.5 hours
Terrain:	Woodland tracks and forest fire rides throughout providing fairly easy walking
Toilets/Refreshments:	Foresters Arms, Fairwarp or Duddleswell Tea Rooms en route
Route:	Fairwarp Church-Duddleswell (Tea Rooms)-Nutley Windmill-Marlpits-Camp Hill-Airman's Grave-Fairwarp Church

A walk in its entirety through Ashdown Forest showing its varying degrees of terrain, from lush undergrowth to wooded ravines to sparse, sandy heathland covered in gorse, bracken and heather. Beginning with the former, the route skirts the little community of Fairwarp before penetrating deeper into the forest along a wide fire ride emerging at the road a little way north of Duddleswell Tea Rooms. The next stage crosses typical Ashdown heathland before crossing another road and heading to the windmill at Nutley. The wooded ravine comes next before another open stretch leading to Camp Hill and the famous radio mast at Duddleswell. Back across the road again to a choice of route, either down a fire ride or through lush ferns to the waterfall and wet heathland both converging on the Airman's Grave before the return to Fairwarp Church.

Directions:

1. *Leave the car park and enter the woods, taking the wider track as far as the T-junction where turn right. In a few yards turn obtusely left along an uneven metalled road, continuing along the footpath as the road peters out.*

2. *Opposite The Cottage bear left into the woods, keeping right at the fork and turning right onto the wide fire ride which follow all the way to the road. (This joins the Wealdway for a short stretch, easily distinguishable by the significant waymarkers as it crosses our route.) At the road the Duddleswell Tea Rooms are about 100 yards (95m) down on the left.*

3. *To continue the walk cross straight over the road and follow the fire ride as it swings round left past the deep valley on the left. About 20 yards (16m) beyond the next fire ride coming up on the left turn right to the road. Cross straight over the road turning left at the next T-junction along a wide ride with extensive views across to the right.*

4. *Take the path through the trees at the Windmill sign, passing through the gate to Nutley Windmill (A). Cross the stile opposite the holly tree, keeping straight ahead across two crossing tracks before turning right at the next fork and skirting the edge of a ravine.*

5. *Once out of the trees keep straight ahead and over the crossing track turning left onto the main track as it sweeps uphill. Cross straight over another crossing track and continue beyond the car park on the right as far as the pond on the left. The area in between used to be an Old Army Camp (B).*

6. *Just past the pond turn right through Hollies car park to the road. Cross straight over road to continue down another wide fire ride and in about 150 yards (140m) there is a choice of route. To visit the waterfall turn right along an obscure path opposite two pine trees. The route soon becomes much wider and more obvious on its way to the waterfall. To continue the walk follow the path left all the way down the valley as far as the left fork just below the houses on the left, crossing the stream by a couple of bridges to rejoin the main route by the Airman's Grave (C). The alternative route keeps straight on down the fire ride.*

7. *Cross over the left of two bridges once past the Airman's Grave noticing how discoloured the stream bed is with the pigment of iron*

Duddleswell Tea Rooms

still. Turn left and left at the next fork keeping left again at the fork by the barn before crossing over at the cross-tracks and continuing to road.

8. *Cross straight over road before turning right almost immediately along a narrow path. Take the right fork behind the house to continue behind the church before turning right at the gravel track back to the car park.*

POINTS OF INTEREST ON THE WALK

(A) Nutley Windmill   see page 47.

(B) Old Army Camp

The Napoleonic Wars left their mark on the area when, in 1793, a great army camp was established on the roadside between Nutley and Duddleswell to meet the threat of revolutionary France, with which Britain was newly at war. Detachments from twelve regiments were housed in the camp, whose site stretched away to the north-east of Duddleswell. A series of mounds in the area, for long time a mystery to archaeologists, have now been identified as the sites of military field kitchens. The area

Airman's Grave

is now shown on the map as Camp Hill as a further reminder of those times, and its 650 ft summit was once crowned with radio masts of which only one now survives. This belongs to the Diplomatic Corps Radio Station, code named Aspidistra during the last war, which broadcast to the continent using the well known Morse Code V to identify it. It also re-transmitted the German Forces programmes and when their radio closed down during RAF raids, Aspidistra broadcast similar music along with German news interspersed with subtle propaganda.

(C) Airman's Grave

A simple stone-walled enclosure in the middle of the track shelters a white cross surrounded by a neat little

Waterfall, near Airman's Grave

garden of remembrance. This is a memorial erected by the mother of Sergeant P.V.R. Sutton, RAF, aged 24, of 142 Bomber Squadron, and five of his comrades who died here when their Wellington bomber crashed after being damaged during a raid on Cologne on July 31, 1941. This is not the original monument, which Mrs Sutton tended regularly until becoming too much for her, and the present memorial was erected in 1972 with money she gave the Conservators for the continued upkeep of "The Grave". Each Remembrance Sunday a wreath from the Conservators is placed by a Ranger, together with one from the Ashdown Forest Riding Association and countless individual poppies are added from members of the public. In 1984 the Air Training Corps became actively involved with the maintenance of the Grave.

WALK 5 - PILTDOWN

A PARISH CHURCH OF ST. BARTHOLOMEW
B HAMMERPONDS
C BARKHAM MANOR VINEYARDS
D FLETCHING

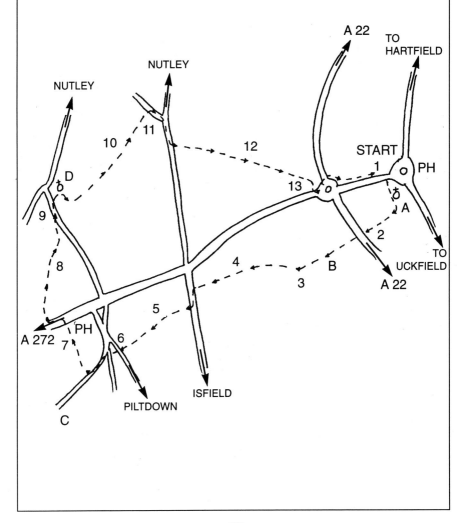

WALK 5 — PILTDOWN

Access/Parking:	Parking off the A272 just opposite the Church
Map Reference:	Landranger 198 grid reference 465240
Distance:	8.5 miles (14km)
Time to Allow:	3 hours
Terrain:	Easy walking along woodland tracks, over the golf course and across open fields
Toilets and Refreshments:	Piltdown Man on the A272. Various venues in Fletching and the Chequers public house in Maresfield
Route:	Maresfield-Park Wood-Piltdown-Barkham Manor (Vineyards)-Fletching-Down Street-Maresfield

This is a walk full of incident; beginning with the unexpected at Park Farm before skirting the remains of the local iron industry's hammerponds and then into the tranquility of Park Wood. Access across Piltdown Golf Course is well indicated before the pleasant approach to Barkham Manor Vineyards and the crossing of the busy A272 to Fletching. The return stretch across open farmland and grazing pastures concludes a very satisfying outing.

Directions:

1. *Cross the A272, through the churchyard of St Barts* (**A**) *then over the stile to cross the field by an obvious route to the lane, where turn right past Park Farm and its unexpected occupants!*
2. *Go over the stile beside the metal gate to continue under the main road then over another stile, keeping ahead along the metalled road past four hammerponds* (**B**) *before taking a fenced path alongside the larger lake.*
3. *Once past the large, modern house, turn right through Park Wood, crossing the bridge over a drain and bearing right in the direction of the yellow waymarker along a broad green lane.*
4. *Keep straight over at the cross-tracks then over a stile to the road. Turn left here and in 100 yards (95m) turn right across Piltdown Golf Course, starting off along a gravel track then keeping ahead along an obvious path as directed by the yellow waymarkers.*
5. *At the marker post offering a choice of direction turn left, then at the 13th tee turn right to the road.*
6. *Turn right here then left at the Public Footpath signpost, bearing*

slightly right at the next fairway to the road. Continue ahead signposted Barkham Manor Vineyard. *At the entrance to Barkham Manor* **(C)** *bear right to the A272. The Piltdown Man public house is about 100 yards (95m) to the right.*

7. *Turn left at the A272 past Old Spot Farm then in 200 yards (190m) turn right along a metalled lane at the low concrete public footpath sign. Follow this lane round right through the farm buildings to follow an obvious route across the fields in the direction of the church spire ahead.*

8. *Through the double gates to turn right along a wide track with a ditch on the right. Keep ahead over two stiles before crossing diagonally left across the playing field to emerge at the road opposite the restored village pump on the outskirts of Fletching* **(D)**

9. *Turn right into the churchyard, turning right to a kissing gate at the southern end bearing left across the next field to cross an unusual stile. Continue ahead to another stile then along a green lane to a third stile.*

10. *Head diagonally right across the next field, crossing a stream and following a well used path before crossing two more stiles and a bridge to a gate to the left of a corrugated building. Continue along a short concrete drive to the road.*

11. *Turn right here and right again at the T-junction. In 200m yards (190m) turn left at the public footpath signpost beside a small pond before taking the right fork across a long field.*

12. *Cross two more stiles before bearing up right across the next field to a stile in the far corner. Continue along a well defined footpath towards the houses ahead, emerging into a private cul-de-sac where keep to the footpath on the left to the road.*

13. *Turn left at the A272, crossing the roundabout back into Maresfield.*

POINTS OF INTEREST ON THE WALK

(A) Parish Church of St Bartholomew see page 34.

(B) Hammerponds

Maresfield once had three ironworks, the last of which was converted into a powder mill in the nineteenth century. This too has now gone but its ponds still remain, now landscaped lakes as seen on the left.

(C) Barkham Manor Vineyards see page 34.

(D) Fletching see page 35.

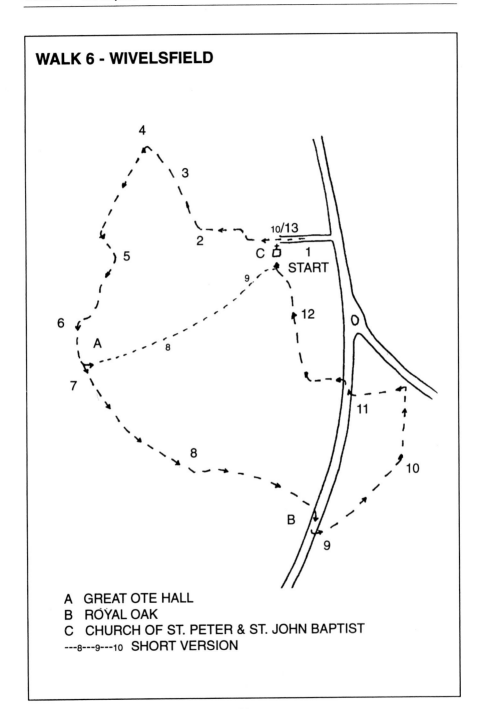

WALK 6 - WIVELSFIELD

A   GREAT OTE HALL
B   ROYAL OAK
C   CHURCH OF ST. PETER & ST. JOHN BAPTIST
---8---9---10 SHORT VERSION

WALK 6 — WIVELSFIELD

Access/Parking:	Car park in the village just before the church
Map Reference:	Landranger 198 grid reference 338208
Distance:	4.25 miles (7km) or 3 miles (4.8km)
Time to Allow:	2 hours (1.25 hours for short walk)
Terrain:	Easy walking along well defined route (which could be muddy after wet weather)
Toilets/Refreshments:	Royal Oak public house (non on short route)
Route:	Wivelsfield-Lunces Common-Theobalds Road-Antye Farm-Great Ote Hall-Royal Oak-Wivelsfield

A very pleasant walk through some lovely Wealdland countryside, beginning with Lunces Hall Estate before dropping down to Theobalds Road, an old Bridleway connecting Burgess Hill and Haywards Heath, two large sprawling urbanisations which practically engulf the entirety of the walk without actually encroaching upon it. Out of nowhere the tall chimneys of Great Ote Hall appear before the decision has to be made whether to cut the walk short or continue on to the Royal Oak public house, which played an important part in the history of this fascinating area. Either route returns to church of St Peter & St John Baptist to conclude this jaunt through easy going countryside.

Directions:

1. *Turn left out of the car park and continue through the white gate and along the drive to Lunces Hall. Immediately before the second gate, turn off right through the kissing gate, continuing alongside the fence on the left.*

2. *Over the stile and down four concrete steps before bearing right across the next field, crossing another stile and then a bridge over a stream before keeping ahead alongside the trees on the left.*

3. *Carry straight on through the farm buildings in the direction of the yellow waymarkers to the pond where continue ahead through the metal gate, keeping alongside the hedge on the right.*

4. *Over the stile to turn left along the wide green lane (Theobalds Road) which eventually becomes a dirt track. Immediately after the interwoven fence of Antye House turn left, over the stile beside the metal gate as the lane swings off right, and keep alongside the fence on the left.*

5. *Turn right at the open field, crossing a double stile before turning left and following the field boundary round to another stile then a plank*

across a ditch.

6. Turn left towards the large house, following the track down to the drive of Great Ote Hall (**A**). Cross the stile beside the 5-barred gate and here decide whether to continue with the full walk or opt for the shortened version.*

7. To continue the full walk, keep alongside the hedge on the right crossing the stile in the bottom corner of the field, keeping alongside the ditch on the left.

8. Cross the bridge to the stile, following the path to the road where turn right to the Royal Oak (**B**).

9. Cross the road with great care, continuing along the Public Bridleway at the far end of the pub car park, following the bridleway through the woods.

10. Turn left over a plank bridge opposite Quinces, then cross a stile before keeping alongside the fence on the right. Over a wooden bridge, keeping ahead across the next field to a stile in the far corner. **D O NOT** cross this stile but turn sharp left alongside a wire fence, passing through three gates to the road.

11. Cross the road and turn right. Immediately after the conifers opposite the garage turn left at the Public Footpath signpost. Keep to the left of the new bungalow before passing right through the rear of the garden, crossing a wide bridge over a deep gully. Turn right over a bridge and a stile then keep straight ahead across the next field.

12. Pass through two squeeze stiles before turning right through a gate into the churchyard of St Peter & St John Baptist (**C**)

13. Turn right at road back to car park

*Short version of the walk:

7. After crossing the stile beside the 5-barred gate, keep alongside the hedge on the left to another stile beside a small copse, then continue along a narrow path which eventually becomes a wide green lane.

8. Over the wide bridge and stile beside another 5-barred gate before crossing diagonally left across the next field and turning sharp right at the stile to continue alongside the hedge on the left.

9. Over a stile then through a squeeze stile to turn left through a gate into the churchyard of St Peter & St John Baptist (**C**)

10. Turn right at road back to car park.

POINTS OF INTEREST ON THE WALK

(A) Great Ote Hall

A fifteenth century manor house which was once the home of Selina Shirley, Countess of Huntingdon, who after being converted to evangelical Methodism had her chaplain proclaim her views to the world.

Another resident, General Shirley, became Commander-in-Chief of forces in North America during the time it was still a British Colony, and, it is said, he never left home without six horses pulling his carriage.

(B) Royal Oak

Here was the scene of a famous murder on May 26th 1734. Jacob Harris, a pedlar, murdered the landlord, his wife and a serving wench, making off with the weeks takings, but he was soon caught and brought to justice. Harris was hanged on August 31st and his body was left to hang on the gibbet near the pub as a warning to others. The area is still known to this day as Jacob's Post and part of the gibbet hangs over the fireplace in the Royal Oak.

It was in the same pub two centuries later a British tradition was established. Jim Dinnage, a local farmer, was drowning his sorrows one

Royal Oak

wet day during hay-making when he spotted a bedraggled donkey outside in the rain. He purchased it and took it home, but it soon fretted for a mate, disturbing most of the villagers with its baying. So farmer Dinnage rescued thirteen similar beasts from the slaughterhouse, persuading a dozen of his friends to each care for a moke and they jokingly became known as The Donkey Club. Farmer Dinnage then had the idea of holding a race meeting to help raise funds to purchase a playing field for the village. It was a huge success but it was felt more donkeys were needed to achieve even greater success. Then Jim Dinnage read in the paper that almost 200 donkeys were running loose after breaking out of a train bound for the slaughterhouse. He took them all in and offered sponsored adoption to the Donkey Club which eventually became a charity. At the next Donkey Derby a staggering 23,000 people attended and a new tradition was established.

(C) Church of St Peter & St John Baptist

It is doubtful there was a church here in Saxon times but there was an early Norman church for the present north doorway is of that date. Older still is the yew tree in the churchyard. Mid way through the thirteenth century the church was largely refashioned and a century later a further enlargement took place. About 1470 the whole church was re-roofed as it is today and covered with Horsham slabs. The south doorway, now the main entrance, was added about this time as was the tower at the west end of the south aisle. The pulpit is Jacobean and was originally of three decks; the font is relatively modern. Registers recording Baptisms, Marriages and Burials are complete from 1559 to present day.

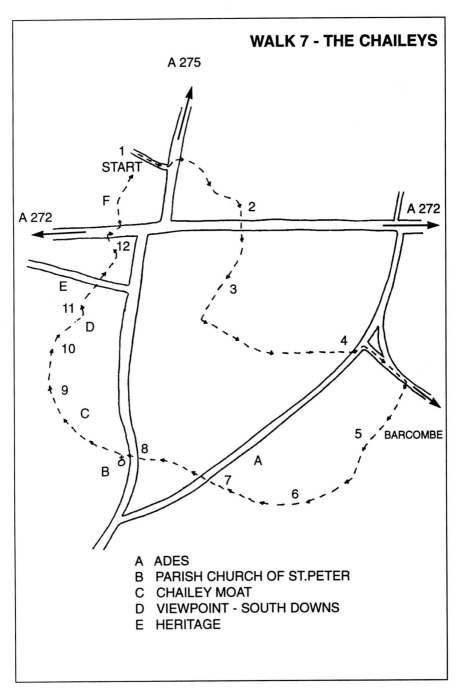

WALK 7 - THE CHAILEYS

A 275

1 START

F

A 272

2

A 272

12

E

3

11

D

10

4

9

C

5 BARCOMBE

8

A

B

7

6

A   ADES
B   PARISH CHURCH OF ST.PETER
C   CHAILEY MOAT
D   VIEWPOINT - SOUTH DOWNS
E   HERITAGE

WALK 7 — THE CHAILEYS

Access/Parking: Red House Common car park, North Chailey, off the A275
Map Reference: Landranger 198 grid reference 392218
Distance: 8 miles (12.8km)
Time to Allow: 3.5 hours
Terrain: Easy walking through farmland, woodland and along well defined paths across open common
Toilets/Refreshments: None on route. The Kings Head public house is about half a mile from the car park at the A272/A275 crossroads
Route: Red House Common-Ades-Chailey Green-Moat-Old Heritage-Chailey Windwill-Red House Common

To walk the whole of Chailey would entail a mammoth trek but this 8 mile (12.8km) circuit envelops the most interesting features of a fascinating area. The north common, from which the walk begins, is reputed to be the centre of Sussex and enjoys an elevated position overlooking the Weald below. Once out of North Chailey the route traverses the old disused railway from Lewes to East Grinstead, part of which further north is the famous Bluebell Railway. The final stretch of the walk, before Chailey Green and the parish church of St Peter, passes the Ades estate while the return route goes through the Old Moat or Parsonage. The concluding section encroaches the north common with the Old Heritage and the Windmill the salient points of interest. All in all it is a walk of contrasts, never hard going and never without interest.

Directions:

1. *Turn right out of the car park to the A275, which cross over before continuing along the drive to Grassington Farm. Pass through a metal gate to the right of the silo (ignoring the main track to the Farmhouse) and continue along a wide track to cross a stream before turning immediately left which eventually becomes Coldharbour Lane.*
2. *Cross over A272 to continue over a stile to follow the path behind the houses before turning sharp right into the woods.*
3. *Cross a stile and then a second stile, continuing ahead to the Public Footpath signpost at the top of the incline. Turn left here, following the footpath to a stile on the left (shortly after the path swings round right). Turn left here over the stile, crossing a large field to a stile in the far right corner.*

4. *Turn left at the road, bearing right at the junction (signposted Barcombe 4 miles). Immediately before Sheepgate Fruit Farm on the left turn right down a track which soon becomes a delightful sunken track. Now continue alongside a long brick wall and into a tree lined track.*

5. *Cross the bridge over Longford Stream, continuing up to where a path crosses. (This section can be very muddy in wet weather). Turn right over the stile here, then over the disused railway, to bear diagonally left across the next field.*

6. *Turn right at the Public Footpath signpost before continuing for a short way along a green track and then bearing left across the next field in the direction of the Public Footpath signpost along a faint path towards the top of the telegraph pole on the skyline. The large house across to the right is Ades* (A)

7. *Over the stile keeping left along the tarmac drive before turning right across the cricket field to the road. Cross straight over road passing to the left of the cottage, over another stile before keeping alongside the fence on the left to the road.*

8. *Cross the road to Chailey Green and the church of St Peter* (B). *Continue along the drive to Chailey Moat* (C), *turning off left by the cattle grid then right over a stile as indicated.*

9. *Over the bridge across a stream, passing though a 5-barred gate to the right, and keeping alongside the fence on the left to a stile. Cross the stile keeping right as waymarked, keeping ahead past the first Public Footpath signpost and turning right into the woods at the second.*

10. *Keep alongside the field boundary on the right, crossing a stile on the right back into the woods* (D)

11. *Turn right at the cross-tracks* (E) *passing the pond on the right before crossing straight over the road, where take the left fork (**NOT** in the direction of the yellow waymarker). In little over 100 yards (95m) bear left along an obvious path across the common to the road, keeping to the left of the houses.*

12. *Turn right into North Chailey then left at the signpost to Chailey Windmill* (F). *Bear right at the barn behind the Windmill back to the car park.*

POINTS OF INTEREST ON THE WALK

(A) Ades

It is a substantial Georgian House built towards the end of the eighteenth century and originally known as Eades. It possibly replaces another house belonging to the family of Richard Ade, who is mentioned around 1308.

(B) Parish Church of St Peter

There was a church here in 1269 according to the earliest documentary evidence available, although it is firmly believed the chancel was built as early as 1250. The tower, the next oldest part, was added in 1280 and it is believed the south aisle was a further addition around 1350. During the next five centuries the church underwent little change until in 1846 when the north aisle was added and a further restoration took place in 1878.

(C) Chailey Moat

Also known in the past as The Parsonage, this house is of great interest because although small moats are not uncommon in the Sussex Weald, it is unusual for the area enclosed to be occupied. Here is a small moated area the entirety of which is covered by a house several centuries old, for the fireplace in one room is thought to date back to 1540. Oak panelling in two principal rooms is of the Elizabethan period. It is thought it became a Rectory in the early eighteenth century, but it is now privately owned and not open to the public.

As to how the moat came to be formed is mere speculation. Rumour has it that it was dug by a Parson in the reign of Queen Anne, although this is most unlikely as it is believed to have been in existence long before that. It is fed by a stream which rises some 3 miles (4.8km) to the south-west at the northern end of the Streat parish, and after passing the house flows under the road at Chailey Green.

(D) Viewpoint — South Downs

To look back towards the South Downs at this point, the massive 'V' is clearly visible made from beech, fir and lime trees; planted in 1887 to commemorate Queen Victoria's golden jubilee.

(E) Heritage

Founded in 1903 from an idea in Juliana Horatia Ewing's book *Story of a Short Life*, Mrs Kimmins arrived at the empty workhouse with seven crippled boys and a heart of gold. Spending a small fortune of her own and a large fortune given by benefactor after benefactor, the colony grew over the years, whereby cripples of both sexes were trained to play an important part in life and become a burden on no-one. Such was the success of the scheme that a second "New" Heritage was opened and Chailey became world famous for its Craft School, producing the finest example of courage, personal belief and willpower the world has ever seen.

(F) Chailey Windmill

The smock mill, which is said to stand in the centre of all Sussex, rightfully belongs to Highbrook, an attractive hamlet 5.5 miles (9km) north of Chailey. Around 1830 it was first erected on a site near the church of St Peter, but about fifteen years later it was moved to Newhaven on the coast to replace a mill which was destroyed by fire. In 1864 it became redundant and was brought back to Chailey to its present site, where it continued its working life until 1911. A considerable amount of money was spent on restoring the mill to working order three years later, but the millstones crashed through the decaying floor and it has remained idle ever since. It was bought on behalf of the Chailey Heritage in 1933 and has been used in several capacities within the School ever since.

Chailey Windmill

WALK 8 - HORSTED HEYNES

A HAMMERPONDS
B BROADHURST MANOR
C HORSTED KEYNES STATION
D ST. GILES CHURCH

WALK 8 — HORSTED KEYNES

Access/Parking:	Car park adjacent to the British Legion and recreational ground at the western end of the village
Map Reference:	Landranger 187 grid reference 384282
Distance:	6 miles (10km)
Time to Allow:	3 hours
Terrain:	Easy walking along well defined paths, on woodland tracks, across open fields and along metalled roads
Toilets/Refreshments:	In Horsted Keynes before or after the walk
Route:	Horsted Keynes-Sussex Border Path-Broadhurst Manor-Tanyard-Horsted Keynes Station-Mill House-Horsted Keynes

This is a must for steam train lovers of all ages, for the Bluebell Railway dominates this walk, which should not detract it in any way for those not so smitten by the age of steam, for it is still a magnificent walk, especially in springtime. Beginning with a peaceful stretch of the Sussex Border Path and its adjacent lakes, it reaches Broadhurst Manor with its animal sanctuary before heading westwards towards the Bluebell Railway and Horsted Keynes station. The return is equally stunning, passing the picturesque Mill House before the gentle stroll back to the fascinating church of St Giles and its interesting churchyard.

Directions:

1. *Cross the road from the car park, continuing down to the right of the Forge along a quiet road to the church. Continue ahead along the Sussex Border Path past the lakes* **(A)** *to Broadhurst Manor* **(B)** *following the main drive as far as the road.*

2. *Turn left at road then right at the T-junction and in 300 yards (285m) left again over the stile at the Sussex Border Path, following the right edge of the next field to a gate into woodland, crossing a bridge over the stream.*

3. *Keep alongside the right perimeter of the next field which follow round left to the fingerpost, turning right into the woods. Follow the Sussex Border Path signs across the wier to bear left across the next field. Cross the stile to the right of the outbuildings to the road, opposite Saxons.*

4. *Turn left at road then right in 100 yards (95m) at Vox End opposite Tanyard Manor, then turn left at the Public Footpath signpost behind*

the outbuildings, following the left edge of the next field with the Bluebell Railway down to the right.

5. *Cross the stiles by the railway bridge, keeping to the left of the track before crossing the line where indicated and turning left alongside it. Follow the obvious route which is well signposted, over the bridge just south of Horsted Keynes station.*

6. *Pass through the gate and along dirt track to visit Horsted Keynes Station (C). Retrace steps to a metal kissing gate over to the right, which leads to a fenced path with woods to the right.*

7. *Turn right at road then left in 100 yards (95m) over the stile opposite Leamland Wood. Follow the path through the woods, turning right at the T-junction beside the lake, then left at the cross-tracks.*

8. *Follow the track round right past Mill House then up to St Giles schoolyard and church (D). Retrace steps back to car park to conclude the walk.*

POINTS OF INTEREST ON THE WALK

(A) Hammerponds

This series of lakes would have been hammerponds during the heyday of the iron industry in Sussex. The furnace was situated in the dip in the road leading from the village to Horsted Keynes railway station and the outflow is a small stream which joins the River Ouse further down.

(B) Broadhurst Manor

Built during the fourteenth century it was the home of the Lord of the Manor and the venue for an amazing discovery of treasure trove half a millenium later. In 1927 a gardener was digging in the garden when his spade struck a crock which broke revealing 64 gold coins, none of which was dated later than 1430. Legend has it that in 1484 Sir Thomas Lewknor, then Lord of the Manor, went off to take part in the War of the Roses, never to return. Perhaps it was he who buried his fortune which is now in the British Museum.

(C) Horsted Keynes Station

This was a junction during British Railways era, with a branch line operating to Haywards Heath until its closure in 1963. There is much here for the visitor to see and enjoy; a period refreshment room, an impressive signal box and a large picnic field. The Bluebell Railway's carriage works are situated here and there is always something of interest standing on the maze of sidings outside the station.

(D) St Giles Church

The church has Saxon and Norman influence and underwent a rebuilding in the thirteenth century. The headless lady brass figure just to the right of the porch dates from the fourteenth century and the church's other interesting feature is the Crusader's Heart Shrine, situated in the Sanctuary just below the altar. Harold MacMillan (later Lord Stockton) one of Britain's leading statesment lived at Birch Grove House nearby and regularly worshipped in St Giles. He died in 1986 and is buried in the eastern section of the churchyard.

S.B. Publications publish a wide range of local interest books on Sussex and other counties.

For a catalogue, please write to:-
S.B. Publications, 19 Grove Road, Seaford, East Sussex BN25 1TP.